Contents

About the Authors v
Authors' Acknowledgments vi
About REA vi

Chapter 1: Introduction 1
   The Common Core State Standards Initiative 2
   What is PARCC®? 3
   Overview of the Literary Analysis Task 3
   Overview of the Research Simulation Task 4
   Overview of the Narrative Task 4

Chapter 2: Literary Analysis Task 7
   Introduction 8
   Practice Session: Reading #1 9
   Practice Session: Reading #2 15
   Practice Session: Reading #3 20
   Practice: Full-Length Literary Analysis Task 24
   More Practice: Full-Length Literary Analysis 32
   Literary Analysis Task: The Essay 37
   Try It Yourself: Essay Question 41

Chapter 3: Research Simulation Task 45
   Introduction 46
   Practice: Identify Text Features #1 48
   Practice: Identify Text Features #2 48
   Practice: Research Simulation Task 50
   Informational Text Sample #1 50
   Informational Text Sample #2 54
   Types of Questions on the Research Simulation Task 58
   Practice: Evidence-Based Selected Response (EBSR) 59
      EBSR Practice #1 61
      EBSR Practice #2 62
      EBSR Practice #3 65
      EBSR Practice #4 67
   Technology-Enhanced Constructed Response (TECR) 69
      TECR Practice #1 70
      TECR Practice #2 71
      TECR Practice #3 71

    Prose-Constructed Response (PCR) 72
        Practice: Prose-Constructed Response. 73
    Practice: Full Research Simulation Task 80

Chapter 4: Narrative Task 89
    Introduction 90
    Evaluating the Narrative Task 91
    Practice Session: Narrative Task. 93
    Narrative Reading Exercise 93
    Narrative Exercise #1 99
    Pre-writing Exercise 101
    Narrative Exercise #2 102

Chapter 5: Practice Tests 1 & 2 105
    Practice Test 1. 107
        Literary Analysis Task 107
        Research Simulation Task. 118
        Narrative Task. 127
    Practice Test 2. 135
        Literary Analysis Task 135
        Research Simulation Task. 144
        Narrative Task. 154

Chapter 6: Answer Keys: Practice Tests 1 & 2 161
    Practice Test 1. 161
        Literary Analysis Task 161
        Research Simulation Task. 163
        Narrative Task. 166
        Writing Task Essay Maps 168
    Practice Test 2. 171
        Literary Analysis Task 171
        Research Simulation Task. 173
        Narrative Task. 175
        Writing Task Essay Maps 177

Appendix A: Graphic Organizers and Charts. 181

Appendix B: PARCC® Literary Analysis, Research Simulation, and Narrative Rubrics 189

Appendix C: PARCC® Technology and Accessibility. 193

Appendix D: Acknowledgments and Credits. 195

About the Authors

Dennis M. Fare, M.Ed.

Dennis M. Fare is the assistant superintendent of the Mahwah Township (N.J.) Public Schools. In 2015, Mahwah students scored above the New Jersey state average on the PARCC® assessments. A sought-after expert on PARCC® implementation, Mr. Fare co-led a presentation at a 2014 Common Core leadership summit. He frequently conducts professional development workshops sponsored by the New Jersey Foundation for Educational Administration. Mr. Fare also is known on the College Board conference circuit, where his topics have included "AP Open Enrollment: From Theory to Praxis," "AP Online Curriculum," and "AP Vertical Teaming: Working from the Ground Up." Mr. Fare has served as an exam reader for AP English Language and Composition and has been a rater for the SAT test.

This book is another in a series of PARCC® ELA test preps Mr. Fare has authored for REA.

Mr. Fare earned a B.A. in English writing and an M.Ed. in English education from Marist College in Poughkeepsie, N.Y. He holds supervisor, principal, and superintendent certifications.

Allison M. Coyle

Allison M. Coyle is an English teacher for the Mahwah (N.J.) Public Schools. She has been an active curriculum developer for the English Department, working to implement PARCC-related techniques while maintaining and fostering an appreciation for classic literature. Ms. Coyle has hosted professional development hours for local teachers, providing insight on how to simultaneously prepare students for standardized tests and continue with instruction as intended. She currently attends Rutgers University–Newark (N.J.), where she is pursuing a master's degree in English with a concentration in women's and gender studies.

Kevin Ulmer, M.A.

Marking his seventeenth year in public education, Kevin Ulmer has worked as a teacher, an assistant principal, and a principal. Currently, he is the principal at George Washington Elementary School in Mahwah, N.J. Under his leadership, George Washington School was named a Reward School for High Performance by the New Jersey Department of Education. Mr. Ulmer has also volunteered with the Middle States Association of Colleges and Schools, conducting peer reviews for accreditation. He is an active member in the National Association for Elementary School Principals; the New Jersey Principal and Supervisors Association; and the Association of Supervision and Curriculum Development. Mr. Ulmer holds a B.A. in elementary and special education from Providence College and an M.A. in educational leadership from Montclair State University.

Authors' Acknowledgments

This book project would not have been possible without the following individuals: Pam Weston, Publisher at REA; Larry B. Kling, Director of Editorial Services at REA; Diane Goldschmidt, Managing Editor at REA; Karen Lamoreux, Developmental Editor; Kathie Gordon, Copyeditor; Kathy Caratozzolo of Caragraphics, Typesetter; and Eve Grinnell, Graphic Designer at REA, for page design and preflight reporting.

We would also like to thank the Mahwah Township Public Schools' administrative team and our teaching colleagues at our respective school districts for sharing their knowledge with us as writers working to make sense of this very new test.

We are grateful to our families, friends, and loved ones for their support during the preparation of this important project. We want to particularly highlight the late Dr. Mark G. Cacciatore, whose love of education and literacy education continues to serve as fuel in creating PARCC® tasks. His passion for language and teaching lives on through these pages.

About REA

Founded in 1959, Research & Education Association (REA) is dedicated to publishing the finest and most effective educational materials—including study guides and test preps—for students of all ages. Today, REA's wide-ranging catalog is a leading resource for students, teachers, and other professionals. Visit *www.rea.com* to see a complete listing of all our titles.

CHAPTER 1

Introduction

Welcome! This book is designed to get you ready to take the Grade 3 PARCC® English Language Arts/Literacy exam. This exam will test your grasp of the third grade English language skills that you need to move ahead. But you might wonder: Why do I need to get ready? Because this exam is probably different from other tests you have taken. You will need to figure things out and put information together on this test, not just answer questions.

This book will give you practice on all the same types of readings, questions, and exercises that you will find on the PARCC® exam. You will find materials to prepare for each of the three tasks included in the test: Literary Analysis, Research Simulation, and Narrative. Chapters 2 through 4 of this book cover each of these three tasks. For each task, you will complete reading and writing exercises similar to the ones you will find on the test. Later, in Chapter 5 of this book, you will find practice tests to get you all ready to take the real one. Chapter 6 contains the answers for both practice tests. In Appendix A at the very back of the book, you will find graphic organizers to help you plan your work. In Appendix B, you will find a rubric that will help you understand what is expected in each task. Be sure to ask your teacher if you need help understanding the rubric. In Appendix C, we cover the technical aspects of the test as well as special accommodations.

In each of the three tasks on the test, you will first read selected pieces of writing, called *texts*. The texts you read in this book will be like the ones you can expect to find on the PARCC® exam. They will include fiction (stories and poetry) and nonfiction (articles and information).

Next, you will answer multiple-choice questions about the texts you have read. These questions sometimes have just one answer, and sometimes more than one. Be sure to read the question very carefully so you will know how many answers there are.

And, finally, there will be a writing assignment in which you will use skills gained from your reading exercises to respond to an essay question using information from the readings.

This pattern is the very same one you will find in each of the three tasks on the PARCC® exam: first readings, then multiple-choice questions, followed by an essay writing assignment. We will include exercises and samples in this book to give you lots of practice for the test.

After you work through the exercises in the review portion of the book, be sure to complete the practice tests in Chapter 5. Also, be sure to use the graphic organizers in Appendix A. These will help you learn how to organize your information.

At times, you may find some of the questions in this book difficult. Don't be afraid to ask your teacher for help when you need it as you go through the readings. As long as you get used to making connections as you read, you'll be able to put that thinking into the essays you will be asked to write.

The PARCC Grade 3 ELA/Literacy Test at a Glance

Task	ELA 1 (Literary Analysis)	ELA 2 (Research Simulation)	ELA 3 (Narrative)
Time	90 minutes	75 minutes	90 minutes

The Common Core State Standards Initiative

This PARCC® test prep is based on the curricular principles of the Common Core State Standards. Each of the tasks and exercises in this book is aligned to those standards. For the first time in U.S. history, the Common Core allows for shared educational expectations that cut across a number of states. In English language arts and in math, the Common Core is a set of rigorous standards that both students and teachers are challenged to meet.

The PARCC® assessment directly reflects the Common Core State Standards. In essence, the PARCC® is designed to assess whether students are making progress toward achieving the benchmarks set forth in the Common Core standards.

This book, therefore, is closely aligned with the PARCC® assessment, and, by extension, with the Common Core standards. For instance, many of the readings you will find in our book are taken from the reading suggestions from the Common Core. Using these reading suggestions will give you an advantage when you take the PARCC® exam. The reason for that advantage is simple: The more familiar you are with the literary and nonfiction texts suggested by the Common Core, the better prepared you will be to take the PARCC® assessment.

We are confident that the reading exercises and activities within this book will give you a running start on the PARCC® exam!

What Is PARCC®?

PARCC® stands for the *Partnership for Assessment of Readiness for College and Careers.* We know—it's a long title! Throughout this test book, we will refer to the exam by its widely known acronym, PARCC®. (In this book, you will see a trademark symbol ® next to the name of the test. A trademark is a brand name, just like Macy's® or McDonald's® or Google®.)

The PARCC® test is unlike any test you probably have ever taken before. Its contents will require both you and your teachers to think in new and exciting ways. Just the fact that you will probably take the exam online using a computer makes it somewhat of a challenge. If you plan to take the exam online, it is very important to look at the practice questions in the context of keyboarding your responses. If you do not yet feel comfortable with keyboarding, now is the time to practice these skills!

Reading activities and these three writing activities will be presented to you when you sit to complete the assessment: (a) a literary analysis essay, (b) a research simulation essay, and (c) a narrative composition. This book will address the reading skills you will need to have, as well as the writing skills necessary for these three types of writing assessments.

Now that you are familiar with the overall structure of the PARCC® exam, let's look over each of the exam's three tasks individually.

Overview of the Literary Analysis Task

The Literary Analysis Task has a 90-minute time limit and may be difficult to organize at first, but with some practice, you'll find that writing this essay can be interesting and fun! You will read multiple texts or view multimedia video clips, and then answer multiple-choice questions that often have two different parts

(Part A and Part B). This will all make more sense to you as you read through these chapters!

The reading passages may consist of any of the following: poems, story excerpts, play excerpts, famous speech passages, or nonfiction article excerpts. After you have read each of the two reading passages, you will be asked to answer multiple-choice questions about the readings, and then to write an essay to compare and contrast them. What does it mean to **compare and contrast**? You will look at some of the **similarities and differences** between the two readings or videos when you start to complete multiple-choice questions and write your essay. It will be your job to make connections between the two texts, and to look at how they are both similar and different.

Overview of the Research Simulation Task

The Research Simulation Task, with a 75-minute time limit, gives you the chance to conduct research! You will work with two different sources of information, which may be shared with you through reading or viewing. The readings or video clips will be connected in some way. Readings or video clips may contain similar characters, messages, or topics. After you read and view these sources, you will be asked to write an essay in which you support your points with information from the readings or videos.

As in the Literary Analysis Task, you will work with readings and videos from many different subject areas. You will learn how to organize your thoughts as you complete your readings and viewings. Then, you will review how to look at a source to choose relevant information as support in your essay. You will learn how to write an essay in which you choose pieces of the information you read to support a conclusion about what you have read.

Overview of the Narrative Task

The Narrative Task will require you to organize your thoughts in a way that is both easy to follow and interesting to read. You will have 90 minutes, or an hour and a half, to complete this task. When most students think of a narrative, they instantly think of a story. This is where the Narrative Task begins. You may read a poem, or a short story, or both, and then use this reading or readings to write a story of your own.

Chapter 1: Introduction

In this task, we will look at organizational strategies and graphic organizers to help you organize your thoughts. Take advantage of the exercises in each of these chapters to increase your organizational abilities, and use the graphic organizers to help you in the pre-writing stages of your essay writing. This task requires you to use your creativity, and you will also need to organize and successfully manage those creative thoughts.

You will need to use your knowledge of **characters** and **setting** to put together a short story, journal entry, or creative essay related to your reading. Let your creativity soar as you put the details from your reading to use in your own creation. Even though this is a test, we want you to have fun thinking and putting your thoughts together. You can do it, and your teacher will help you along the way.

 A Starting Tip: Be sure to pre-plan your writing! We cannot say it enough: Pre-writing before you begin writing is a very important practice. Get used to pre-writing with *all* types of writing.

Reading and writing are fun. Enjoy the adventure!

Let's get started!

CHAPTER 2

Literary Analysis Task

Task Time: 90 minutes

A Message to Educators and Parents

The Literary Analysis Task of the Grade 3 PARCC® English Language Arts/Literacy Assessment gives students 90 minutes to complete three steps:

1. Reading
2. Answering multiple-choice questions
3. Writing an essay

Students begin by reading two works of literature or informational articles between 200 and 800 words each. These pieces include short stories, poems, and other grade-level works of fiction or informational text.

After each reading, students answer multiple-choice questions about the passages. Each of these question sets has two parts: Part A and Part B. Part A tests students on a particular detail of the short story, requiring students to demonstrate the skills of vocabulary acquisition, character analysis, and theme identification. Part B asks students to support their answers to Part A by choosing direct evidence from the text.

The culminating task for students in the Literary Analysis Task asks them to write an analytical essay on an overarching topic that relates to both reading passages. The passages will be linked in some way; for example, by a similar moral message or by a particular type of character. Students will have to respond to a question using specific details from each of the texts, illustrating the connections that they have made between the two.

This chapter is aligned with the following Common Core standards:

CCSS.ELA-Literacy.RL.3.1	CCSS.ELA-Literacy.L.3.1
CCSS.ELA-Literacy.RL.3.2	CCSS.ELA-Literacy.L.3.2
CCSS.ELA-Literacy.RL.3.3	CCSS.ELA-Literacy.L.3.3
CCSS.ELA-Literacy.RL.3.4	CCSS.ELA-Literacy.L.3.4
CCSS.ELA-Literacy.RL.3.5	CCSS.ELA-Literacy.L.3.5
CCSS.ELA-Literacy.RL.3.6	CCSS.ELA-Literacy.W.3.1
CCSS.ELA-Literacy.RL.3.7	CCSS.ELA-Literacy.W.3.2
CCSS.ELA-Literacy.RL.3.8	CCSS.ELA-Literacy.W.3.3
CCSS.ELA-Literacy.RL.3.9	CCSS.ELA-Literacy.W.3.4
CCSS.ELA-Literacy.RL.3.10	CCSS.ELA-Literacy.W.3.5
CCSS.ELA-Literacy.RF.3.4	CCSS.ELA-Literacy.W.3.6

Introduction

The Literary Analysis Task in the PARCC® test is much like a treasure hunt. For this particular kind of treasure hunt, imagine that you will have (1) two treasure maps, (2) a handful of clues, and (3) a final reward. Your treasure maps are two short stories, and your clues are multiple-choice questions that make you think and will lead you to great discoveries. The treasure comes at the end of your journey, when you write an essay combining what you have learned from all of those multiple-choice question clues along the way. You will have a chance to practice this treasure hunt in the Practice Session later on.

Here are the three steps of your "treasure hunt" in the Literary Analysis Task that you will find on the PARCC® test.

Step 1: Read the two provided pieces of writing. Think of them as treasure maps. On a real treasure hunt, a map is the source that you can always look back to when you need direction. The text you read serves the same purpose for the Literary Analysis Task.

As you read each piece of writing, imagine the steps you would take if you were searching for treasure using a map. A successful treasure hunter marks up the map, circles important points, and makes notes to come back to later. You should do the same with each of the readings. Read them very closely, paying attention to what the characters are like, marking difficult words, and taking note of any events that seem important to the story.

Chapter 2: Literary Analysis Task

Step 2: Answer the multiple-choice questions that follow. They are clues that will allow you to successfully complete your treasure hunt. They make you think about big ideas from the story—and those big ideas will show up in the final essay question. Each question also acts as a guide, asking you to pick out important details from the story and to support your answers.

When you get to the second text, repeat steps 1 and 2.

Step 3: Write an essay. The essay is the end point of the treasure hunt—the destination to which the maps and clues have led you. The essay question will ask you to think about the two readings very closely. You will have to look back at what you have learned about the characters and the overall message of the readings. You will need to review your clues to guide you in the right direction. You can gather information from those treasure map stories, and talk about details from them in your essay to support your answer.

You will have a whole 90 minutes, or an hour and a half, for this journey. If you follow the steps carefully, you will be sure to successfully complete the treasure hunt!

Practice Session

Reading #1

Read through the following excerpt from Ruth Stiles Gannett's *My Father's Dragon*. As you read, underline important parts of the text to remind yourself of important details.

Remember that each of the stories is like a guiding treasure map. A treasure map will lead you to the gold—but only if you actively follow each of the steps and really examine each bit of the map. The same goes for each of the stories you will read. You need to be an active seeker. Active seekers ask themselves questions and make notes while they read. Every time you read a story, it is a journey, and a journey requires you to be active. This time, it is your mind getting in on the action! Review the questions below, and then give it a try yourself.

Ask yourself these questions while you read:

1. **Who are the main characters?**
   What makes this person (or animal) who he or she is? For example: Is he or she bossy, kind, smart, lazy, etc.?

2. **What is the main message of the story?**
   What have you learned from reading it? What details in the story have helped to get this message across?

3. **What vocabulary words are difficult?**
   What words are new to you? Underline any words you do not recognize. Then look at the other words and phrases around the difficult words to help you come up with a definition for each unfamiliar word.

Passage from Chapter 7, "My Father Meets a Lion,"
from *My Father's Dragon,* by Ruth Stiles Gannett

1 "Who are you?" the lion yelled at my father. "My name is Elmer Elevator."

2 "Where do you think you are going?"

3 "I'm going home," said my father.

4 "That's what you think!" said the lion. "Ordinarily I'd save you for afternoon tea, but I happen to be upset enough and hungry enough to eat you right now." And he picked up my father in his front paws to feel how fat he was.

5 My father said, "Oh, please, Lion, before you eat me, tell me why you are so particularly upset today."

6 "It's my mane," said the lion, as he was figuring out how many bites a little boy would make. "You see what a dreadful mess it is, and I don't seem to be able to do anything about it. My mother is coming over on the dragon this afternoon, and if she sees me this way I'm afraid she'll stop my allowance. She can't stand messy manes! But I'm going to eat you now, so it won't make any difference to you."

7 "Oh, wait a minute," said my father, "and I'll give you just the things you need to make your mane tidy and beautiful. I have them here in my pack."

Chapter 2: Literary Analysis Task

8 "You do?" said the lion. "Well, give them to me, and perhaps I'll save you for afternoon tea after all," and he put my father down on the ground.

9 My father opened the pack and took out the comb and the brush and the seven hair ribbons of different colors. "Look," he said, "I'll show you what to do on your forelock, where you can watch me. First you brush a while, and then you comb, and then you brush again until all the twigs and snarls are gone. Then you divide it up into three and braid it like this and tie a ribbon around the end."

10 As my father was doing this, the lion watched very carefully and began to look much happier. When my father tied the ribbon he was all smiles. "Oh, that's wonderful, really wonderful!" said the lion. "Let me have the comb and brush and see if I can do it." So my father gave him the comb and brush and the lion began busily grooming his mane. As a matter of fact, he was so busy that he didn't even know when my father left.

 **Questions**

Let's look at a few multiple-choice questions about the passage you just read.

1. Part A

What does the word dreadful mean as it is used in paragraph 6 of this chapter from *My Father's Dragon*?

Ⓐ lovely

Ⓑ painful

Ⓒ silly

Ⓓ terrible

Part B

Which detail best supports the answer to Part A?

Ⓐ " '. . . if she sees me this way I'm afraid she'll stop my allowance. She can't stand messy manes!' " (paragraph 6)

Ⓑ " 'But I'm going to eat you now, so it won't make any difference to you.' " (paragraph 6)

Ⓒ ". . . he was figuring out how many bites a little boy would make." (paragraph 6)

Ⓓ " '. . . I'll give you just the things to make your mane tidy and beautiful.' " (paragraph 7)

2. Part A

How do the details in the story show the idea of cleverness?

Ⓐ through describing the lion's fear of his mother's reaction

Ⓑ through his father's words and actions

Ⓒ through the explanation of the lion's anger

Ⓓ through the father's list of objects in his pack

Part B

Which line from the text best supports the answer to Part A?

Ⓐ " 'I'm going home,' said my father." (paragraph 3)

Ⓑ " '. . . I happen to be upset enough and hungry enough to eat you right now.' " (paragraph 4)

Ⓒ " 'My mother is coming over on the dragon this afternoon, and if she sees me this way I'm afraid she'll stop my allowance.' " (paragraph 6)

Ⓓ "As my father was doing this, the lion watched very carefully and began to look much happier." (paragraph 10)

3. Part A

Read this sentence from paragraph 9 of the story:

> "My father opened the pack and took out the comb and the brush and the seven hair ribbons of different colors."

Why does the father take out a comb, brush, and ribbons?

Ⓐ He wants to show off how good he is at maintaining manes.

Ⓑ He wants to distract the lion so that he does not eat him.

Ⓒ He wants to please the lion's mother.

Ⓓ He cannot stand a messy mane.

Part B

Which detail from this chapter from *My Father's Dragon* shows another example of the answer to Part A?

Ⓐ " 'Oh, please, Lion, before you eat me, tell me why you are so particularly upset today.' " (paragraph 5)

Ⓑ " 'She can't stand messy manes!' " (paragraph 6)

Ⓒ " 'You see what a dreadful mess it is, and I don't seem to be able to do anything about it.' " (paragraph 6)

Ⓓ ". . . he put my father down on the ground." (paragraph 8)

Answer Key

1. Part A

When you answer this question, first cross out any positive (or good) words, because we know that the lion is very upset about his messy mane. This eliminates "lovely" (A) and "silly" (C). Now you have a 50/50 chance of getting to the correct answer! We know that the messy mane causes problems for the lion because he is nervous about seeing his mother, but there is no clue that makes us think that the mane is "painful" (C); it is just not very pretty. And it makes the lion feel "terrible" (D). **The best choice is answer D: terrible.**

Part B

Now that you know the answer to Part A is D (terrible), you need to look back to the story—your treasure map—for the detail that led to that definition. Answer choices B and D have more to do with the lion's desire to eat the father than they do with the word *terrible*, so you can eliminate those choices. In answer choice C, the father offers a way to make the lion's situation less terrible, so that cannot be the answer. **Only answer choice A lets us know that terrible things are happening because of his messy mane!**

2. Part A

The first thing to ask yourself is: What is *cleverness*? Once you remember that if a person is *clever*, it means he or she uses intelligence and skill to make problems better, you can move forward. So, the question is asking: How does a person make a problem better by being intelligent? Answer choices A and C talk about parts of the story that make the problem worse, so those cannot be correct. Answer choice D might at first seem to be the one, but in thinking further we realize that a list of objects cannot in themselves make a problem better. Since the story is all about how a person uses those things, we are led to B. The father uses his words to distract the lion, and he uses the actions of brushing the mane so that the lion forgets to eat him. **The best answer is B.**

Part B

Now, you need to look for a detail to show that the father said or did something to help solve the problem of the lion eating him. Right away, you should eliminate B and C because they show what the lion says and does, not what the father says and does. Answer choice A shows the father wanting to go home, but it does not show him finding a way to get there. So, we have to go with D because it shows the father distracting the lion by showing him how to take care of his mane. This is a way he uses his smarts to avoid becoming the lion's lunch. **The best answer is D.**

3. Part A

This is a question that asks you to look back at your notes about who all of the characters are. Answer choice A does not fit anything we know about the father; he has not proven himself to be a person who cares about showing off, so we can eliminate this answer. Answer choices C and D might be true, but we do not have any details from the text that would support these ideas. We know that the main thing the father needs to do is keep from becoming a lion's meal, so we settle on B. **The best answer is B.**

Part B

Part B asks you to think about the ways the father has attempted to avoid being eaten. What has he done and what has he said to stay alive? Answer choice A is the only choice that shows the father doing something to distract the lion. He asks the lion why he feels so bad, so that the lion will (hopefully) forget all about eating him. None of the other details show the father trying to avoid being eaten. **The best answer is A.**

Reading #2

Read through the following excerpt from Mary Pope Osborne's *The One-Eyed Giant (*Book 1 of *Tales from the Odyssey). * As you read, underline important points to remind yourself of important details.

Remember that this story is like a treasure map. It will lead you to the gold—but only if you actively follow each of the steps and really examine each bit of the map. As you read the story, you need to be an active seeker. Active seekers ask themselves questions and make notes while they read. Every time you read a story, it is a journey, and a journey requires you to be active. This time, it is your mind getting in on the action! Review the questions below and then give it a try yourself.

Ask yourself these questions while you read:

1. **Who are the main characters?**
   What makes this person (or animal) who he or she is? For example: Is he or she bossy, kind, smart, lazy, etc.?

2. **What is the main message of the story?**
   In other words, what have you learned from reading this story? What details in the story have helped to get this message across?

3. **What vocabulary words are difficult?**
   Underline any words you do not recognize. Then look at the other words and phrases around the difficult words to help you come up with a definition for each word you do not know.

Passage from Chapter 5, "The One-Eyed Giant"

from *The One-Eyed Giant* (Book 1 of *Tales from the Odyssey*) by Mary Pope Osborne

1 A hideous giant lumbered into the clearing. He carried nearly half a forest's worth of wood on his back. His monstrous head jutted from his body like a shaggy mountain peak. A single eye bulged in the center of his forehead.

2 The monster was Polyphemus. He was the most savage of all the Cyclopes, a race of fierce one-eyed giants who lived without laws or leader. The Cyclopes were ruthless creatures who were known to capture and devour any sailors who happened near their shores.

3 Polyphemus threw down his pile of wood. As it crashed to the ground, Odysseus and his men fled to the darkest corners of the cave.

4 Unaware that the Greeks were hiding inside, Polyphemus drove his animals into the cave. Then he rolled a huge boulder over its mouth to block out the light of day and imprison his flock inside.

5 Twenty-four wagons could not haul that rock away, Odysseus thought desperately. How will we escape this monster?

6 Odysseus' men trembled with terror as the giant made a small fire and milked his goats in the shadowy light. His milking done, he threw more wood on his fire. The flame blazed brightly, lighting up the corners of the cave where Odysseus and his men were hiding.

7 "What's this? Who are you? From where do you come?" the giant boomed. He glared at the Greeks with his single eye. "Are you pirates who steal the treasure of others?"

8 Odysseus' men were frozen with terror. But Odysseus hid his own fear and stepped toward the monster.

9 "We are not pirates," he said, "We are Greeks blown off course by storm winds. Will you offer us the gift of hospitality like a good host? If you do, mighty Zeus, king of the gods, will be pleased. Zeus is the guardian of all strangers."

10 "Fool!" the giant growled. "Who are you to tell me to please Zeus? I am a son of Poseidon, god of the seas! I am not afraid of Zeus!"

11 Odysseus' men cowered in fear.

12 Polyphemus moved closer to Odysseus. He spoke in a soft, terrible voice. "But tell me, stranger, where is your ship? Near or far from shore?"

Chapter 2: Literary Analysis Task 17

13 Odysseus knew Polyphemus was trying to trap him. "Our ship was destroyed in the storm," he lied. "It was dashed against the rocks. With these good men I escaped, I ask you again, will you welcome us?"

Questions

1. Part A

What is the meaning of the word **ruthless** as it is used in paragraph 2 of "The One-Eyed Giant"?

- Ⓐ ugly
- Ⓑ intelligent
- Ⓒ cruel
- Ⓓ irresponsible

Part B

Which detail from the story **best** supports your answer to Part A?

- Ⓐ "His monstrous head jutted from his body like a shaggy mountain peak." (paragraph 1)
- Ⓑ "A single eye bulged in the center of his forehead." (paragraph 1)
- Ⓒ "... lived without laws or leader..." (paragraph 2)
- Ⓓ "... known to capture and devour any sailors who happened near their shores." (paragraph 2)

2. Part A

Which of the following characteristics **best** describes Odysseus' men?

- Ⓐ brave
- Ⓑ mean
- Ⓒ hungry
- Ⓓ afraid

Part B

Which line from the story best shows that Odysseus is different from his men?

Ⓐ "Odysseus' men trembled with terror..." (paragraph 6)

Ⓑ "But Odysseus hid his own fear and stepped toward the monster." (paragraph 8)

Ⓒ "'We are Greeks blown off course by storm winds.'" (paragraph 9)

Ⓓ "Odysseus knew Polyphemus was trying to trap him." (paragraph 13)

3. Choose the two best details that show that Odysseus is brave and put them into the chart below.

1.	2.

Ⓐ Odysseus thinks about how to escape the monster.

Ⓑ Odysseus and his men hide.

Ⓒ Odysseus questions the monster's manners.

Ⓓ Odysseus steps toward the monster.

 **Answer Key**

1. Part A

The word *ruthless* describes the Cyclopes. After reading a little bit about them, you should see that they are very mean beings. They eat men just for showing up on their island! You should eliminate answer choice A because the details about what the Cyclopes look like are not near the word *ruthless*. You will find that, most of the time, the clues about the word's meaning are very near to it. Answer choice B can be eliminated, because the Cyclopes are never seen as smart—just mean. Answer choice D might seem like the right answer, but, by devouring men and capturing men, the Cyclopes are more cruel than they are irresponsible. **The best answer is C.**

Chapter 2: Literary Analysis Task

Part B
Answer choice D should stand out to you, as it shows the Cyclopes using their power to do really mean and violent things to visitors, such as eating them upon arrival! Answer choice C lets us know that the Cyclopes do not have a whole lot of leadership or guidance; but that does not mean that they are definitely cruel beings. Answer choices A and B describe the Cyclopes' outer appearance, and we know that we cannot judge a book by its cover, so those details do not tell us much about the Cyclopes' personalities. **The best answer is D.**

2. Part A
Odysseus' men are seen hiding in fear in a few different scenes in the story, so we know that they are not answer choice A (brave). They do not behave in a way that makes us think that they are mean, so we can also eliminate answer choice B. We might start to assume that the men are hungry if they have been trapped in the cave, but the one word that describes them best has to be **afraid. The best choice is answer D.**

Part B
You know you are looking for something that shows Odysseus as someone who is not like his men—someone who is not afraid. Answer choice A describes Odysseus' men and does not tell us anything about Odysseus, so that can be eliminated right away. Answer choices C and D let us know that Odysseus is very aware of the danger he faces, but they do not really show that he is brave. Answer choice B is a direct example of Odysseus showing that he is brave. **The best answer is B.**

3. Answer choice A shows Odysseus on the track to showing bravery—but just thinking of how to solve the problem does not show bravery as well as some of the other answer options. Answer choice B does not show bravery at all, as Odysseus hides with his men. Answer choices C and D show Odysseus standing up to the monster even though we know just how scary the giant is from the description of him. These are the two best details that show that Odysseus is brave.

| C. Odysseus questions the monster's manners. | D. Odysseus steps toward the monster. |

Reading #3

Read through the following poem, "A Bat Is Born," by Randall Jarrell. As you read, mark up the text to remind yourself of important details.

Remember that each of the stories is like a guiding treasure map. A treasure map will lead you to gold—but only if you actively follow each of the steps and really examine each bit of the map. The same goes for each of the stories you will read. You need to be an active seeker. Active seekers ask themselves questions and make notes while they read. Every time you read a story, it is a journey, and a journey requires you to be active. This time, it is your mind getting in on the action! Review the questions below, and then give it a try yourself.

Ask yourself these questions while you read:

1. **Who are the main characters?**
   What makes this person (or animal) who he or she is? For example: Is he or she bossy, kind, smart, lazy, etc.?

2. **What is the main message of the story?**
   In other words, what have you learned from reading this?
   What details in the story have helped to get this message across?

3. **What vocabulary words are difficult?**
   Underline them. Look at the other words and phrases around them to help you come up with a definition.

Poem: "A Bat Is Born," from *The Bat-Poet*
By Randall Jarrell

A bat is born
Naked and blind and pale.
His mother makes a pocket of her tail
And catches him. He clings to her long fur
5 By his thumbs and toes and teeth.
And then the mother dances through the night
Doubling and looping, soaring, somersaulting—
Her baby hangs on underneath.
All night, in happiness, she hunts and flies
10 Her sharp cries
Like shining needlepoints of sound

Go out into the night and, echoing back,
Tell her what they have touched.
She hears how far it is, how big it is,
15 Which way it's going:
She lives by hearing.
The mother eats the moths and gnats she catches
In full flight; in full flight
The mother drinks the water of the pond
20 She skims across. Her baby hangs on tight.
Her baby drinks the milk she makes him
In moonlight or starlight, in mid-air.
Their single shadow, printed on the moon
Or fluttering across the stars,
25 Whirls on all night; at daybreak
The tired mother flaps home to her rafter.
The others are all there.
They hang themselves up by their toes,
They wrap themselves in their brown wings.
30 Bunched upside down, they sleep in air.
Their sharp ears, their sharp teeth, their quick sharp faces
Are dull and slow and mild.
All the bright day, as the mother sleeps,
She folds her wings about her sleeping child.

 **Questions**

1. **Part A**

   Reread lines 1 through 2: "A bat is born/ Naked and blind and pale." What is the most important thing this tells us about the baby bat?

   Ⓐ He is sick.

   Ⓑ He needs his mother.

   Ⓒ He cannot fly.

   Ⓓ He needs shelter.

Part B

What other line from the text supports the idea in Part A?

- Ⓐ "All night, in happiness, she hunts and flies" (line 9)
- Ⓑ "She lives by hearing" (line 16)
- Ⓒ "The mother eats the moths and gnats she catches" (line 17)
- Ⓓ "Her baby hangs on tight" (line 20)

2. **Part A**

Which word best describes the mother's feelings while she takes care of her new baby?

- Ⓐ glad
- Ⓑ tired
- Ⓒ nervous
- Ⓓ bored

Part B

Which line from the poem supports the answer to Part A?

- Ⓐ "All night, in happiness, she hunts and flies" (line 9)
- Ⓑ "She hears how far it is, how big it is" (line 14)
- Ⓒ "The tired mother flaps home to her rafter" (line 26)
- Ⓓ "She folds her wings about her sleeping child" (line 34)

Chapter 2: Literary Analysis Task

3. **Which lines from the poem help to show the close bond between the mother and her baby?**

   Ⓐ "His mother makes a pocket of her tail/And catches him. He clings to her long fur" (lines 3–4)

   Ⓑ "And then the mother dances through the night/Doubling and looping, soaring, somersaulting" (lines 6–7)

   Ⓒ "In moonlight or starlight, in mid-air./ Their single shadow, printed on the moon" (lines 22–23)

   Ⓓ "They hang themselves up by their toes" (line 28)

   Ⓔ "She folds her wings about her sleeping child." (line 34)

| 1. | 2. | 3. |

Answer Key

1. Part A

Answer choices A and C are not things that we can just assume about the bat. It might be true that he is sick or cannot fly, but those details do not quite lead us to that answer. Answer choice D might also be true, but the baby needs more than just shelter. Picture a tiny and helpless little creature. It is clear that he needs the love and care of his mother. **The best answer is B.**

Part B

Now you know you are looking for a detail that shows that the baby needs his mother. Answer choices A, B, and C all let us know about the mother bat's behavior, but not about what the baby is doing. Answer choice D shows us that the baby bat clings to his mother and needs her to hold him. **The best answer is D.**

2. Part A

This is a tricky question, but you should notice that the word **best** appears in the question. Mother bat might be feeling a lot of different things, but it is up to you to decide which feeling describes her the best. We know that mother is tired (B) after she hunts all night, but this does not really fully show how she feels about caring for her newborn baby—imagine the joy a mom feels caring for her child! She might be tired, but her joy is even stronger, which is why the best answer is A. Mother bat dances through the sky and happily holds her baby all the while. The details that show her as a happy mother are more important than the details that show that she is tired. Answer choices C and D do not have any support in the text. **The best answer is A.**

Part B
Now it is time to look for a detail that shows that the mother is glad. Answer choice A is the only choice that really shows the happiness that the mother feels while taking care of her baby. **The best answer is A.**

3.

A. "His mother makes a pocket of her tail/And catches him. He clings to her long fur" (lines 3–4)	C. "In moonlight or starlight, in mid-air./Their single shadow, printed on the moon" (lines 22–23)	E. "She folds her wings about her sleeping child." (line 34)

Answer choice B talks only about the mother, so it does not tell you much about the relationship between mother **and** baby bat. Answer choice D talks about the other bats nearby and does not give information on mother and baby. **The best answers are A, C,** and **E** because they all show the closeness, both physical and emotional, that mother and baby share.

Practice: Full-Length Literary Analysis Task

Now, you will read two stories, "Tops and Bottoms" by Janet Stevens and "How the Camel Got His Hump" by Rudyard Kipling. Up until now in this Practice Session, you have read just one reading at a time. But in the PARCC® test that you are preparing to take, you will generally find two readings placed together, each one followed by multiple-choice questions, and then an essay question relating to *both* readings.

So get your thinking cap on, and try the full-length format of the Literary Analysis Task here. First, read both pieces of writing below and answer the questions, and then you will be asked to write an essay.

Tip: As you read, think about the lessons that the characters in the stories have learned, and take some notes. This will help you understand the theme of the stories and be better prepared to answer the essay question that follows the readings.

Tops and Bottoms
By Janet Stevens

1 Once upon a time there lived a very lazy bear who had lots of money and lots of land. His father had been a hard worker and a smart business bear, and he had given all of his wealth to his son.

2 But all Bear wanted to do was sleep.

3 Not far down the road lived a hare. Although Hare was clever, he sometimes got into trouble. He had once owned land, too, but now he had nothing. He had lost a risky bet with a tortoise and had sold all of his land to Bear to pay off the debt.

4 Hare and his family were in very bad shape.

5 "The children are so hungry, Father Hare! We must think of something!" Mrs. Hare cried one day. So Hare and Mrs. Hare put their heads together and cooked up a plan.

6 The next day Hare hopped down the road to Bear's house. Bear, of course, was asleep.

7 "Hello, Bear, wake up! It's your neighbor, Hare, and I have an idea!"

8 Bear opened one eye and grunted.

9 "We can be business partners!" Hare said. "All we need is this field right here in front of your house. I'll do the hard work of planting and harvesting, and we can split the profit right down the middle. Yes, sir, Bear, we're in this together. I'll work and you sleep."

10 "Huh?" said Bear.

11 "So, what will it be, Bear?" asked Hare. "The top half or the bottom half? It's up to you—tops or bottoms."

12 "Uh, let's see," Bear said with a yawn. "I'll take the top half, Hare. Right—tops."

13 Hare smiled. "It's a done deal, Bear."

14 So Bear went back to sleep, and Hare and his family went to work. Hare planted, Mrs. Hare watered, and everyone weeded.

15 Bear slept as the crops grew.

16 When it was time for the harvest, Hare called out, "Wake up, Bear! You get the tops and I get the bottoms."

17 Hare and his family dug up the carrots, the radishes, and the beets. Hare plucked off all the tops, tossed them into a pile for Bear, and put the bottoms aside for himself.

18 Bear stared at his pile. "But, Hare, all the best parts are in your half!"

19 "You chose the tops, Bear," Hare said.

20 "Now, Hare, you've tricked me. You plant this field again—and this season I want the bottoms!"

21 Hare agreed. "It's a done deal, Bear."

22 So Bear went back to sleep, and Hare and his family went to work. They planted, watered, and weeded.

23 Bear slept as the crops grew.

24 When it was time for the harvest, Hare called out, "Wake up, Bear! You get the bottoms and I get the tops."

25 Hare and his family gathered up the lettuce, the broccoli, and the celery. Hare pulled off the bottoms for Bear and put the tops in his own pile.

26 Bear looked at his pile and scowled. "Hare, you have cheated me again."

27 "But, Bear," Hare said, "you wanted the bottoms this time."

28 Bear growled, "You plant this field again, Hare. You've tricked me twice, and you owe me one season of both tops and bottoms!"

29 "You're right, poor old Bear," sighed Hare. "It's only fair that you get both tops and bottoms this time. It's a done deal, Bear."

30 So Bear went back to sleep, and Hare and his family went to work. They planted, watered, and weeded, then watered and weeded some more.

31 Bear slept as the crops grew.

32 When it was time for the harvest, Hare called out, "Wake up, Bear! This time you get the tops and the bottoms!"

33 There in front of Bear's house lay a high field of corn. Hare and his family yanked up every cornstalk. Hare tugged off the roots at the bottom and the

tassels at the top and put them in a pile for Bear. Then he carefully collected the ears of corn in the middle and placed them in his own pile.

34 Bear rubbed his eyes and watched.

35 "See, Bear? You get the tops and the bottoms. I get the middles. Yes, sir, Bear. It's a done deal!"

36 By now Bear was wide awake. "That's it, Hare!" he hollered. "From now on I'll plant my own crops and take the tops, bottoms, and middles!"

37 Hare and his family scooped up the corn and hopped down the road toward home.

38 Bear never again slept through a season of planting and harvesting. Hare bought back his land with the profit from the crops, and he and Mrs. Hare opened a vegetable stand.

39 And although Hare and Bear learned to live happily as neighbors, they never became business partners again!

Questions

1. **Part A**

    What is the meaning of the phrase cooked up as it is used in paragraph 5?

    Ⓐ destroyed

    Ⓑ baked

    Ⓒ developed

    Ⓓ imagined

Part B
Which line from the text best supports your answer to Part A?

Ⓐ "Hare and his family were in very bad shape." (paragraph 4)

Ⓑ "The children are so hungry, Father Hare!" (paragraph 5)

Ⓒ "Bear opened one eye and grunted." (paragraph 8)

Ⓓ " 'We can be business partners!' Hare said. 'All we need is this field right here in front of your house. I'll do the hard work of planting and harvesting, and we can split the profit right down the middle. Yes, sir, Bear, we're in this together. I'll work and you sleep.' " (paragraph 9)

2. Part A
In "Tops and Bottoms," Hare and Bear behave very differently from one another. Which of the following characteristics describes Hare and does not describe Bear?

Ⓐ lazy

Ⓑ angry

Ⓒ hardworking

Ⓓ wealthy

Part B
Which of the following lines best supports your answer to Part A?

Ⓐ "Bear slept as the crops grew." (paragraph 15)

Ⓑ "Hare called out, 'Wake up, Bear! You get the tops and I get the bottoms.' " (paragraph 16)

Ⓒ "Bear stared at his pile. 'But, Hare, all the best parts are in your half!' " (paragraph 18)

Ⓓ ". . . Hare and his family went to work. They planted, watered, and weeded, then watered and weeded some more." (paragraph 30)

3. Part A
Which detail from the story **best** supports the idea that one must work for what one has?

- Ⓐ Bear's father leaves him a lot of money.
- Ⓑ Bear continues to lose his crops until he takes care of their growth himself.
- Ⓒ Hare tricks Bear into taking the worst parts of the vegetables.
- Ⓓ Bear gets angry when he realizes that Hare has fooled him.

Part B
What evidence from the story illustrates the acceptance of this important lesson?

- Ⓐ "So Bear went back to sleep, and Hare and his family went to work. Hare planted, Mrs. Hare watered, and everyone weeded." (paragraph 14)
- Ⓑ "Bear growled, 'You plant this field again, Hare. You've tricked me twice, and you owe me one season of both tops and bottoms!'" (paragraph 28)
- Ⓒ "'You're right, poor old Bear,' sighed Hare. 'It's only fair that you get both tops and bottoms this time. It's a done deal, Bear.'" (paragraph 29)
- Ⓓ "'That's it, Hare!' he hollered. 'From now on I'll plant my own crops and take the tops, bottoms, and middles!' . . . Bear never again slept through a season of planting and harvesting." (paragraph 36)

 **Answer Key**

1. Part A
"Cooked up" is used in paragraph 5 when Mr. and Mrs. Hare talk about what they will do next in order to feed their hungry family. We know that they will not (A) destroy a plan because then they would not have a plan to feed their hungry children! (B) baked might sound like what "cooked up" would mean, but we know that Mr. and Mrs. Hare are making a plan, not food, in this moment. Finally, "imagined" (D) is too weak of an answer. Hare goes beyond imagining and actually develops (C) a plan that he can use to help feed his family. **The best answer is C: developed.**

Part B

From answering Part A, you know that Hare is developing a plan. To answer Part B, you need to decide which part of the story helps to show that. Answer choices B, C, and D do not have any mention of a plan, but A tells us exactly how Hare plans to feed his family—by tricking Bear! **The best answer is A.**

2. Part A

This question can be tricky if you are not careful in your note-taking. Make sure you keep each of the characters separate in your mind and write down important characteristics of each one. We know that "lazy" (A) cannot be the answer because Hare is out planting and watering all day! "Angry" (B) is a weak answer because there is no part of the story that shows Hare as angry, and "wealthy" (D) is the exact opposite of Hare, who struggles to feed his family! **The best answer is C: hardworking.**

Part B

In Part B, you need to find the answer that supports Hare as a hard worker. Answer choice B has nothing to do with Hare as a worker. It might show him as tricky, but that is it. Answer choices A and C describe Bear. You need to be careful when the question asks you about one character but provides descriptions about another. Bear is seen as lazy in answer choice A, but that does not actually tell you anything about Hare. **The best answer is D: ". . . Hare and his family went back to work. They planted, watered, and weeded, then watered and weeded some more."**

3. Part A

The question asks you to find a detail from the text that shows that hard work is important. Answer A could not possibly be the right answer because Bear did not have to work hard for his dad to leave him any money. Answer C supports that Hare is tricky and that Bear should pay attention to what is going on around him, but it does not say anything about hard work. Answer D is not correct because Bear's anger does not show that a person (or a bear) needs to work. It just shows that he does not like to be fooled. It is only once Bear realizes that he will never have his own crops again unless he plants them himself that he learns his lesson. **The best answer is B: Bear continues to lose his crops until he takes care of their growth himself.**

Part B

You know you are looking for a line that supports the idea that Bear will plant his own crops from now on. Answer choice C is simply another moment in

Chapter 2: Literary Analysis Task

which Hare tricks Bear, so that does not show Bear learning his lesson. Answer choice B shows Bear's anger but not that he has learned his lesson, and choice A cannot be correct because it shows the opposite of hard work—Bear takes a nap! **The best answer is D: "'That's it, Hare!' he hollered. 'From now on I'll plant my own crops and take the tops, bottoms, and middles!' . . . Bear never again slept through a season of planting and harvesting."**

Take a Break

This is a good place to stop and think about the work that you have done so far. You have *almost* completed steps 1 and 2 of the treasure hunt! Do you remember what those steps are? That's right:

Step 1: Read the provided text.

Step 2: Answer the multiple-choice questions that follow.

You have just one more story to go before you move on to the essay question. You're almost there!

You have already read three other passages in the Practice Session of this chapter and answered a number of multiple-choice questions. So, it should be crystal clear why note-taking while you read is so important. Can you remember why? That's right: The multiple-choice questions and your answers contain important clues about how you will answer the essay question at the end. Think of the multiple-choice questions and answers as the building blocks for your essay. Your notes along the way will help you remember which blocks to use!

Writing down a few simple notes about each of the characters can be very helpful—such as that Hare is the one who is willing to work, and Bear is the one who would rather sleep. Then you will use those notes to help you answer the essay question. For example, the multiple-choice questions about the "Tops and Bottoms" reading have asked you about the behavior of characters in the story, and how the characters managed to learn a certain lesson. Taking notes about who the characters are and what they learned will help you when you come to write your essay.

More Practice: Full-Length Literary Analysis

Now read the second story below. Pay close attention to who the characters are and what they do. Remember to take notes during your reading! You will be asked to write the essay after you have read the story and answered the questions.

How the Camel Got His Hump
By Rudyard Kipling

1 In the beginning of years, when the world was so new and all, and the Animals were just beginning to work for Man, there was a Camel, and he lived in the middle of a Howling Desert because he did not want to work; and besides, he was a Howler himself. So he ate sticks and thorns and tamarisks and milkweed and prickles, most 'scruciating idle; and when anybody spoke to him he said 'Humph!' Just 'Humph!' and no more.

2 Presently the Horse came to him on Monday morning, with a saddle on his back and a bit in his mouth, and said, 'Camel, O Camel, come out and trot like the rest of us.'

3 'Humph!' said the Camel; and the Horse went away and told the Man.

4 Presently the Dog came to him, with a stick in his mouth, and said, 'Camel, O Camel, come and fetch and carry like the rest of us.'

5 'Humph!' said the Camel; and the Dog went away and told the Man.

6 Presently the Ox came to him, with the yoke on his neck and said, 'Camel, O Camel, come and plough like the rest of us.'

7 'Humph!' said the Camel; and the Ox went away and told the Man.

8 At the end of the day the Man called the Horse and the Dog and the Ox together, and said, 'Three, O Three, I'm very sorry for you (with the world so new-and-all); but that Humph-thing in the Desert can't work, or he would have been here by now, so I am going to leave him alone, and you must work double-time to make up for it.'

9 That made the Three very angry (with the world so new-and-all), and they held a palaver, and an indaba, and a punchayet, and a pow-wow on the edge of the Desert; and the Camel came chewing on milkweed most 'scruciating idle, and laughed at them. Then he said 'Humph!' and went away again.

Chapter 2: Literary Analysis Task

10 Presently there came along the Djinn in charge of All Deserts, rolling in a cloud of dust (Djinns always travel that way because it is Magic), and he stopped to palaver and pow-pow with the Three.

11 'Djinn of All Deserts,' said the Horse, 'is it right for any one to be idle, with the world so new-and-all?'

12 'Certainly not,' said the Djinn.

13 'Well,' said the Horse, 'there's a thing in the middle of your Howling Desert (and he's a Howler himself) with a long neck and long legs, and he hasn't done a stroke of work since Monday morning. He won't trot.'

14 'Whew!' said the Djinn, whistling, 'that's my Camel, for all the gold in Arabia! What does he say about it?'

15 'He says "Humph!" said the Dog; 'and he won't fetch and carry.'

16 'Does he say anything else?'

17 'Only "Humph!"; and he won't plough,' said the Ox.

18 'Very good,' said the Djinn. 'I'll humph him if you will kindly wait a minute.'

19 The Djinn rolled himself up in his dust-cloak, and took a bearing across the desert, and found the Camel most 'scruciatingly idle, looking at his own reflection in a pool of water.

20 'My long and bubbling friend,' said the Djinn, 'what's this I hear of your doing no work, with the world so new-and-all?'

21 'Humph!' said the Camel.

22 The Djinn sat down, with his chin in his hand, and began to think a Great Magic, while the Camel looked at his own reflection in the pool of water.

23 'You've given the Three extra work ever since Monday morning, all on account of your 'scruciating idleness,' said the Djinn; and he went on thinking Magics, with his chin in his hand.

24 'Humph!' said the Camel.

25 'I shouldn't say that again if I were you,' said the Djinn; you might say it once too often. Bubbles, I want you to work.'

26 And the Camel said 'Humph!' again; but no sooner had he said it than he saw his back, that he was so proud of, puffing up and puffing up into a great big lolloping humph.

27 'Do you see that?' said the Djinn. 'That's your very own humph that you've brought upon your very own self by not working. Today is Thursday, and you've done no work since Monday, when the work began. Now you are going to work.'

28 'How can I,' said the Camel, 'with this humph on my back?'

29 'That's made a-purpose,' said the Djinn, 'all because you missed those three days. You will be able to work now for three days without eating, because you can live on your humph; and don't you ever say I never did anything for you. Come out of the Desert and go to the Three, and behave. Humph yourself!'

30 And the Camel humphed himself, humph and all, and went away to join the Three. And from that day to this the Camel always wears a humph (we call it 'hump' now, not to hurt his feelings); but he has never yet caught up with the three days that he missed at the beginning of the world, and he has never yet learned how to behave.

 **Questions**

1. Part A

What does the phrase most 'scrutiating idle mean as it is used in paragraph 1?

- Ⓐ rude
- Ⓑ lazy
- Ⓒ busy
- Ⓓ loud

Part B

Which line from the story best supports your answer to Part A?

- Ⓐ "... he did not want to work ..." (paragraph 1)
- Ⓑ "... he ate sticks and thorns and tamarisks and milkweed and prickles ..." (paragraph 1)
- Ⓒ "... he was a Howler himself ..." (paragraph 1)
- Ⓓ "... when anybody spoke to him he said 'Humph!'" (paragraph 1)

Chapter 2: Literary Analysis Task 35

2. **Part A**
   Which word **best** describes Djinn's feelings about Camel?

   Ⓐ supportive

   Ⓑ understanding

   Ⓒ sad

   Ⓓ angry

   Part B
   Which line from the story **best** supports your answer to Part A?

   Ⓐ " 'Very good,' said the Djinn." (paragraph 18)

   Ⓑ " 'My long and bubbling friend,' said the Djinn, 'what's this I hear of your doing no work, with the world so new-and-all?' " (paragraph 20)

   Ⓒ "The Djinn sat down, with his chin in his hand . . ." (paragraph 22)

   Ⓓ ". . . 'don't you ever say I never did anything for you. Come out of the Desert and go to the Three, and behave. Humph yourself!' " (paragraph 29)

3. **The Horse, the Ox, the Dog, and the Djinn try to get the Camel to stop being so lazy. Fill in the three most important steps from the list below that Horse, Ox, Dog, and Djinn take to get Camel to work, in the order in which they happen in the story.**

   Ⓐ Djinn gives Camel a hump.

   Ⓑ Horse, Ox, and Dog tell Djinn about Camel's lack of work.

   Ⓒ Djinn sees Camel looking at himself in a pool of water.

   Ⓓ Horse, Ox, and Dog ask Camel to help them with their work.

   Ⓔ Camel says, "Humph!"

   Ⓕ Djinn makes Horse, Ox, and Dog make up for Camel's absence.

1.
2.
3.

 **Answer Key**

1. Part A
In paragraph 1, we meet the "most 'scruciating idle" Camel. While we know he is "rude" (A), the phrase does not refer to when Camel just says "Humph!" in reply to everything. He is considered idle because he does not want to move or work. The best way to describe the way he acts is "lazy" (B). **The best answer is B: lazy.**

Part B
Which detail helps to show a very lazy camel? Answer choices B, C, and D show some unpleasant behaviors, but only answer choice A shows Camel's true laziness! **The best answer is A: ". . . he did not want to work . . ." (paragraph 1).**

2. Part A
When the Djinn finds out that the Camel has not been working, he plans for the Camel's punishment. A person who is supportive or understanding would not jump to this action. The Djinn does not show sadness when he punishes the Camel. He really just shows anger, and that is how the camel got his hump. **The best answer is D: angry.**

Part B
Now we need evidence of Djinn's anger. Answer choices A and C do not show an angry Djinn at all. Answer choice B shows us the start of Djinn's frustration with Camel, but it is not until Camel "Humphs" at Djinn that his true anger is shown (in answer D). **The best answer is D: ". . . 'don't you ever say I never did anything for you. Come out of the Desert and go to the Three, and behave. Humph yourself!'" (paragraph 29).**

Chapter 2: Literary Analysis Task

3.

D. Horse, Ox, and Dog ask Camel to help them with their work.
B. Horse, Ox, and Dog tell Djinn about Camel's lack of work.
A. Djinn gives Camel a hump.

This question is asking you to show the steps that finally got the Camel to stop being 'scruciating idle. Answer choices C, E, and F do not directly lead up to the end of the Camel's laziness. Once you know the three actions that answer the question best, it is up to you to look back to the story to see the order that they show up in. Make sure you take note of what happened first, second, and last.

Literary Analysis Task: The Essay

Remember, the essay is the final challenge you have been working toward. This is your end treasure. It will really show if you have paid close attention to the clues along the way, and if you have taken in the information from the two readings.

The essay question will always ask you about both readings. It is your job to combine information from each of the two readings to answer one overarching or central, question.

Tip: Here are two important points to remember:
1. Make sure to answer all parts of the essay question.
2. Use details that come directly from the two readings.

Think of the readings as guides to answering all of the questions. You can and should look back to them for guidance, just as you would check a map on a treasure hunt.

Below the essay question here, you will find some tips to help you in this final goal: writing your essay. You will not find these tips on the test, however. Then you will be on your own. So take the time to learn them now!

Essay Question

Hare and Djinn both teach characters an important lesson in the stories. Write an essay that explains how Hare and Djinn's words and actions are important to the overall teaching of the lesson in the stories. Use what you have learned about the characters to support your answers.

Tips: Before answering the question, really think about what the task is asking you to do. One tip is to *label* the actual question with *numbers*, so that you do not forget any parts of the question when you begin the writing and planning process.

For this particular question, you should notice that you need to do the following.

1. Identify an important lesson that connects both of the stories.
2. Show how Hare's words relate to the lesson.
3. Show how Djinn's words relate to the lesson.
4. Show how Hare's actions relate to the lesson.
5. Show how Djinn's actions relate to the lesson.

Label the Essay Question with these numbers. Then, use them in your planning process to make sure you do not forget any parts of the question.

So, your planning process will look like this:

Step 1: Label the Essay Question.

Hare and Djinn both teach characters **an important lesson (1)** in the stories.

Write an essay that explains how **Hare and Djinn's words (2, 3) and actions (4, 5)** are important to the overall teaching of the lesson in the stories. Use what you have learned about the characters to support your answers.

Step 2: Make a table or chart that helps you to organize your information.

If you are a student who learns better from seeing rather than hearing, this step will be very helpful for you! See a sample chart below.

Chapter 2: Literary Analysis Task

	Lesson (1)	**Words (2, 3)**	**Actions (4, 5)**
Hare	If you are lazy, bad things will happen to you. Note: Another way to word this would be: If you are hardworking, good things will happen to you.	Look for something Hare has said that helps Bear to learn the lesson listed in the lesson column. **(2)** **Detail:** Hare says, " 'You chose the tops, Bear' " after Bear screams that Hare has all of the good parts of the crops. **(2A)** **Explain:** Hare's words teach the lesson. Hare points out to Bear that his lazy ways have caused him to lose out on the good parts of the crop. Because Bear was lazy, he never even asked what it meant to have the tops. **(2B)**	Look for something Hare has done that helps Bear to learn the lesson listed in the lesson column. **(4)** **Detail:** Hare's trick throughout the whole story is what makes Bear wake up and realize that he needs to plant his own crops. **(4A)** **Explain:** By showing Bear that it takes work to create good plants, Hare teaches Bear to stop being lazy. **(4B)**
Djinn		Look for something Djinn has said that helps Camel to learn the lesson listed in the lesson column. **(3)** **Detail:** Djinn says to Camel, "Do you see that? That's your very own humph that you've brought upon your very own self by not working." **(3A)** **Explain:** Djinn's words teach the lesson. Djinn wants Camel to know that the hump is from his own laziness. **(3B)**	Look for something Djinn has done that helps Camel learn the lesson listed in the first column. **(5)** **Detail:** Djinn puts a hump on Camel's back that he joins the rest of the animals in their work. **(5A)** **Explain:** Even though Camel never ends up liking the work, the hump is what forces him to stop being lazy. **(5B)**

After you complete a detailed chart, the writing process becomes very easy because all of the most important parts of your essay are already filled out for you. Once your chart is complete, you just have to build the essay up from there.

Start with a **topic sentence** that tells us what your whole essay is about. Then, use the information from your chart to support that first sentence. You will see in the sample below why it is so important to work hard on your chart. A well-done chart leads to a well-done essay.

Sample Response to Essay Question

Both Hare and Djinn use words and actions to show Bear and Camel that **being lazy will cause bad things to happen (1)**. **Hare and Djinn's words** show Bear and Camel that you cannot be lazy if you want to have a good life **(2, 3)**. After Bear gets the worst parts of the plants, Hare tells Bear that he is the one who chose to have those parts. Hare says, "'You chose the tops, Bear,'" after Bear screams that Hare has all of the good parts of the crops **(2A)**. The reason Bear picks the tops is that he is too lazy to plant on his own, and he is even too lazy to ask about what it means to have the tops **(2B)**. When Hare reminds Bear that he is the one who chose the bad parts, he is also reminding him that his laziness has caused something bad to happen. Just like Hare, Djinn uses words to prove to Camel that his laziness is wrong. Djinn says to the Camel, "Do you see that? That's your very own humph that you've brought upon your very own self by not working" **(3A)**. Djinn wants the Camel to notice that it is his own fault that he has been given a hump. He wants Camel to know that his hump is from his own laziness. Both Hare and Djinn use words to teach that bad things happen when you are lazy **(3B)**.

Note: **Hare and Djinn also use actions (4, 5)** to teach the main lesson about the importance of hard work. Hare's trick throughout the whole story is what makes Bear wake up and realize that he needs to plant his own crops **(4A)**. By showing Bear that it takes work to create good plants, Hare teaches Bear to stop being lazy **(4B)**. Djinn's actions also teach Camel an important lesson. It is not until Djinn puts a hump on the Camel's back that he joins the rest of the animals in their work **(5A)**. Even though Camel never ends up liking the work, the hump is what forces him to stop being lazy **(5B)**. If Hare and Djinn never took action, Bear and Camel never would have changed.

Try it Yourself

This is your chance to show off all you have learned! You are now ready to go for this end goal on your own. Write your own essay answering the Essay Question below.

Essay Question

Bear and Camel both learn from their bad behavior. Write an essay that explains how Bear and Camel's words and actions show what they have learned from their bad behavior. Use what you have learned about the characters to support your answers.

Tip: Remember to take the two steps to planning your essay—before you write!
1. Label the actual prompt with numbers.
2. Make a table or chart that helps you to organize your information. If you are a student who learns better from seeing rather than hearing, this step will be very helpful for you.

Getting Started on the Essay

1. **Label the Prompt.**

    Bear and the Camel both **learn from their bad behavior (1)**.

    Write an essay that explains how **Bear and the Camel's words (2, 3)** and **actions (4, 5)** show how they have learned from their bad behavior. Use what you have learned about the characters to support your answers.

2. **Chart it out** on the following page.

	Lesson (1)	Words (2, 3)	Actions (4, 5)
Bear	Bear and Camel learn that if you are lazy, you will not succeed.	2A Detail: 2B Explanation:	4A Detail: 4B Explanation:
Camel		3A Detail: 3B Explanation:	5A Detail: 5B Explanation:

3. Write the Essay. Once you have put all of your information in the chart, write the essay in a way that answers each part of the question, trying your very best to show just how much of an expert you have become on these stories!

You can use the PARCC® Literary Analysis and Research Rubric in Appendix B in the back of this book to see just how well you have done!

CHAPTER 3

Research Simulation Task

Task Time: 75 minutes

A Message to Educators and Parents

The second task that third grade students are challenged with in the PARCC® English Language Arts/Literacy Assessment is the Research Simulation Task. Understandably, the name of the task itself may bring on feelings of uncertainty and nervousness for both teachers and students.

Let's face it: most third grade students are only in the early stages of conducting any type of formal research, and much of their previous research has been done through experience and not through the use of texts, pictures, diagrams, and videos. The "All About" books that are commonly written by students in K–2 classrooms are often based on what a student thinks he or she knows about a particular topic, rather than on research-based facts.

Although text complexity has been raised to a new level in the PARCC® assessment, you will find that many of the skills for which third grade students need to demonstrate mastery in the Research Simulation task are skills that have already been introduced and have been part of classroom instruction in most third grade classrooms well before PARCC®.

This chapter is aligned with the following Common Core standards:

CCSS.ELA-Literacy.RI.3.1	CCSS.ELA-Literacy.L.3.1
CCSS.ELA-Literacy.RI.3.2	CCSS.ELA-Literacy.L.3.2
CCSS.ELA-Literacy.RI.3.3	CCSS.ELA-Literacy.L.3.3
CCSS.ELA-Literacy.RI.3.4	CCSS.ELA-Literacy.L.3.4
CCSS.ELA-Literacy.RI.3.5	CCSS.ELA-Literacy.L.3.5
CCSS.ELA-Literacy.RI.3.6	CCSS.ELA-Literacy.W.3.1
CCSS.ELA-Literacy.RI.3.7	CCSS.ELA-Literacy.W.3.2
CCSS.ELA-Literacy.RI.3.8	CCSS.ELA-Literacy.W.3.3
CCSS.ELA-Literacy.RI.3.9	CCSS.ELA-Literacy.W.3.4
CCSS.ELA-Literacy.RI.3.10	CCSS.ELA-Literacy.W.3.5
CCSS.ELA-Literacy.RF.3.4	CCSS.ELA-Literacy.W.3.6

Introduction

In this chapter, you will explore the second part of the PARCC® ELA/Literacy test. It is called the Research Simulation Task (RST), which can sound scary at first. It sounds so complicated! But there is no need to feel scared or nervous. This task is easier than its big name makes it sound, and this chapter will guide you every step of the way.

This task is intended to do exactly what the name suggests: *simulate* research. "Simulate" means to imitate, or do something in a similar way. So in this task, you will *simulate* research. This task does not expect or require you to do in-depth research to be successful.

What to Expect on the RST

The Research Simulation Task that you will face in the PARCC® Assessment is called the "RST" for short. Questions on the RST will require that you have the following skills. Hopefully, after seeing this list, you can relax. You've done all of this before! None of these skills are totally new to your third grade classroom.

- Use context clues.

- Find the main idea.

- Compare and contrast.

- Draw conclusions.

Chapter 3: Research Simulation Task

- Make inferences.

- Support your answers with evidence from the text.

Here's what you'll do in this chapter to get ready to take the RST portion of the PARCC® test:

- Use texts and pictures to conduct your research.

- Use multiple sources to shape your thoughts.

- Practice and sharpen the skills that you will need in the RST.

The RST focuses on the use of informational, or nonfiction texts. The term "informational text" is used because these texts provide information and facts. Informational texts come in different forms, including articles, essays, books, and speeches. Regardless of the type of informational text that you are reading, there will always be a main idea and evidence to support the main idea. Each nonfiction reading will provide you with new information on a given topic. It is important that you use the information provided by the source as evidence when completing the research questions.

Informational Text Structure

To make information easier to understand, authors often use a specific structure when creating informational texts. Most likely, the informational texts that you read will have a structure that falls under one of the following four categories:

1. Cause and Effect (the reason something happens and the result that follows)
2. Chronological Order (events in the order that they happened)
3. Compare and Contrast (similarities and differences)
4. Problem and Solution (a problem and how it can be or was solved)

In order to be successful on the Research Simulation Task, you will need to be familiar with informational (nonfiction) texts and the text features that they commonly use. Here are eight common nonfiction text features that you may find on the PARCC®:

- Titles

- Headings

- Sub-headings

- Pictures

- Bold print

- Italics

- Captions

- Labels

These text features are used to help readers understand what they are reading. They also help readers move, or "navigate," through an informational piece of writing (which is often called a "source" in research). It is important that you can correctly identify the information text features because the terms for these features will be used in questions on the PARCC® test. So to understand the questions, you will need to know the names of these features. You will also need to be able to navigate through the text on the PARCC® test and use the text features.

Practice: Identify Text Features #1

When you look at nonfiction passages and works, take a look at each one of the text features mentioned above.

Practice: Identify Text Features #2

An easy way to continue to practice identifying text features is to flip through nonfiction books and place sticky notes next to each text feature. This will allow you to see text features used in different locations on a page and make sure you can correctly identify each feature.

Make sure you can do each one of the following activities. When you can, you will have no problem understanding the questions on the RST.

1. **Tell the difference between a line and a paragraph.** It is important that you understand the difference between a *line* and *a paragraph*. This is important because on the PARCC®, some readings are organized by *lines*, and others by *paragraphs*. It is very important that you can tell the difference, so that you will understand which one the question is asking about.

2. **Be able to find a specific line or paragraph in the text.** The PARCC® test often mentions a particular line or paragraph in a question, or in the multiple-choice responses. You must be able to find that same line or paragraph in the text in order to answer the question. You had some practice in the previous chapter finding words and parts of sentences in the text, so you are probably pretty good at this!

3. **Be able to find a specific phrase in the text.** Usually, when you are asked to support your answer with a phrase from the text, a paragraph number is provided to assist you in locating the phrase. This should make it fairly easy to find the phrases that are listed as answer choices. When you select a phrase, it is important that you consider only the words listed in the answer choice, and not in the entire sentence containing the answer choice.

Practice: Research Simulation Task

When preparing for the Research Simulation Task (RST), you will be faced with the challenge of how to organize and keep track of your thoughts. There are many different ways to do this, but it is always best to keep the process as simple as possible. One possible method is to use graphic organizers with multiple shapes, or come up with "acronyms" that provide clues to help you remember the text. (An acronym is a series of letters; for example, "RWA" would help you remember the phrase: "reading, writing, arithmetic.") Although these techniques work, they sometimes make you confused. You might get caught up worrying about what each letter stands for or which organizer to use, instead of focusing on the task at hand.

In most cases, the simpler the organizer, the better. A simple T-chart is a useful planning tool for the RST. A "T-chart" is a type of **chart**, or graphic organizer, in which you make vertical columns with headings across the top of the page and rows of information in rows and columns underneath. In your T-chart, you will fill in the chart with information that you gather from the reading. This method allows you to quickly write down your thoughts when reading. It also provides an easy visual cue to help you compare and contrast. This chapter uses a T-chart format to annotate readings and present a reader's possible thought process. You can use the end product as a reference when practicing for the RST.

> **Teacher's Note**
> Although Venn diagrams are also useful for comparing and contrasting texts (and may be seen as Technology-Enhanced Constructed Responses), younger students often have trouble writing within the confines of the circles, making the end result of their work hard to read.

Informational Text Sample #1

Let's look together at an informational text and see how you would read it in preparation for the RST. Below this informational text, you will find tips and suggestions for how to read the passage. After that, you will read a second informational text on your own.

Plant Life Cycles

By Anita Ganeri

Nature's Patterns

1 Nature is always changing. Many of the changes that happen follow a **pattern**. This means that they happen over and over again.

2 Plant life cycles follow a pattern. A **seed** grows, makes more seeds, and finally dies. Then the new seeds grow and make their own seeds. The cycle starts again.

New Plants

3 There are many different kinds of plants. But most of them will grow in the same way. Most new plants have a life cycle that starts with a **seed**.

4 New plants **sprout** from seeds. Some plants grow very quickly. Other plants grow slowly. Trees are plants that can take many years to grow to their full size.

Growing Seeds

5 Most **seeds** grow in soil. They start to grow into plants under the soil. When a seed starts to grow, this is called **germination**.

6 First, the hard case around the seed breaks open. Then, a root grows down into the soil. A first shoot grows up and the plant's first leaves begin to open.

Rambling Roots

7 A plant's roots grow at the bottom of its **stem**. They are usually hidden under the soil. The roots hold the plant in place so that it does not blow over.

8 As the roots grow, they get longer and spread out through the soil. There are tiny hairs at the end of each root. These hairs soak up water and **nutrients** from the soil.

Leaves and Food

9 Plants need food to live and grow. Animals must find food to eat, but plants can make their own. Plants make their food in their leaves. This is called **photosynthesis**.

10 A plant's leaves collect sunlight. They use it to mix **gas** from the air with water from the soil. Inside the leaves, the gas and water are turned into sugary food for the plant.

Strong Stems

11 A plant's leaves grow out of its **stem**. Some stems grow tall and strong. Other stems grow along the ground or curl around other plants for support.

12 There are lots of tiny tubes inside the stem. Some tubes carry water from the roots to the leaves. Other tubes carry food from the leaves all around the plant.

Blooming Flowers

13 Some plants grow flowers at the end of the **stems**. Other plants have flowers all along their stems. Flowers make **seeds** that grow into plants.

14 A flower grows from a **bud**. Most buds are small and green. They burst open to show their flowers. Many plants flower in the spring and summer.

Inside a Flower

15 There are many different parts inside a flower. These parts make the plant's **seeds**. One part of the flower makes a powdery dust called pollen.

16 Pollen travels from one flower to another. It joins with part of the new flower to make a seed. Sometimes the wind blows the pollen. Sometimes birds or insects carry it.

Sprouting Seeds

17 A **seed** starts to grow inside the flower. Once the flower has made a seed, its job is finished. Its petals **droop** and fall off, and the flower dies.

18 Inside the seed are the parts that will grow into a new plant. The seed also stores food that the new plant can use to grow.

Before reading, ask yourself a few questions to help spark your thought process:

1. What is the main idea of the text?
2. What information is the author providing for me?
3. Why is the author giving me this information?

It is also important to look at the text features (that is, how the text is presented, or treated) to gather as much information as possible before reading. Here are some of the text features you will find in an informational text.

1. **Titles.** The title may or may not give you information about the main idea of the text. In this case, it certainly does. The title "Plant Life Cycles" immediately tells you what you will be learning about in the text.

2. **Sections.** At first glance, you can see that this text is divided into sections. Each section has a heading written in bold print. These headings give you clues as to what each section will be about.

3. **Bold print.** Notice that there are words within each section that are written in bold print. This is a clue that these words are important. As the reader, you need to make sure that you pay close attention to these words and do your best to understand their meaning. The word "seed(s)" appears in bold print many times in the text. This suggests that the seed is an important part of the plant life cycle and is something you should pay close attention to as you read.

4. **Labels.** Authors often provide diagrams with labels in nonfiction texts Diagrams can be used to help you understand the information the author provides in the text. See a sample diagram below.

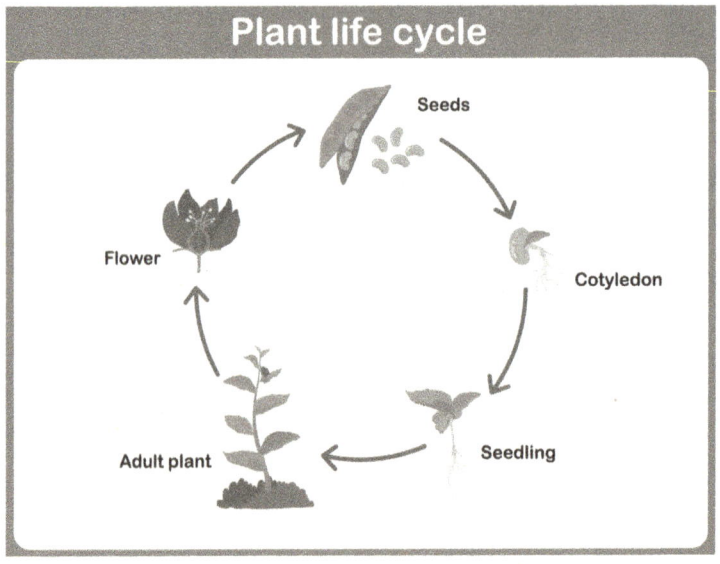

Chapter 3: Research Simulation Task

It is important that you actively engage in thought when you read. As you work through the text, jot down your thoughts on a T-chart. For example, here is some important information in the "Plant Life Cycles" reading, which you would probably want to record on your T-chart. See the T-chart below:

Text Sample #1 Plant Life Cycles	Text Sample #2
• The pattern is: 　1. Seed grows 　2. Makes new seeds 　3. Dies • Most plants grow the same way • A plant's life starts with a seed • Some plants grow fast others grow slow • Most seeds grow under the ground • Plants grow up and down. The roots go down and the stem and leaves go up • Roots help the plant stay in the ground • Plants need food • Plants can make their own food • The stem carries food to the plant • A flower's job is to make a seed	

After reading, you will want to look to see if you can answer the three questions you asked yourself before you began to read.

1. What is the main idea of the text?
   The text is mainly about the life cycle of a plant.

2. What information is the author providing for me?
   The author is providing me with information about how a plant grows.

3. Why is the author giving me this information?
   The author wants me to understand how a plant can grow from a seed and that most plants have the same growing process.

Informational Text Sample #2

Now that you've reviewed the steps to successfully reading an informational text, try reading one on your own.

Remember the steps you practiced above:

Step 1. Ask yourself these questions before reading.

1. What is the main idea of the text?
2. What information is the author providing me?
3. Why is the author giving me this information?

Step 2. Take notice of the different text features.

Step 3. Write down your thoughts on the T-chart on page 53 as you read.*

*****Teachers and parents:** For this exercise, it would be helpful to provide your students with a copy of the T-chart on page 53.

Animal Life Cycles—Growing and Changing

By Bobbie Kalman

Animal life cycles

1 Animals are living things. Living things breathe, eat, grow, and change. There are many kinds of animals. Some are tiny, and others are huge! As animals grow, they go through many stages, or sets of changes. The stages that animals go through make up their life cycles. Different animals have different life cycles.

Changing animals

2 Animals are born or hatch from eggs. The animals then grow and change into adults. Adult animals are fully grown and can make babies on their own.

Growing embryos

3 When animals begin to grow, they are called **embryos**. Some embryos grow inside the bodies of their mothers. Other embryos grow inside eggs that are laid by their mothers.

Some animals are born

4 Animal mothers that have embryos growing inside their bodies are pregnant. When an embryo has finished growing, it is born. It leaves its mother's body.

Breaking out

5 Embryos that do not grow inside the bodies of their mothers grow inside eggs that were laid by their mothers. When the embryos have grown enough, they **hatch**. To hatch is to break out of an egg. Babies that hatch from eggs are called hatchlings.

Growing up

6 Young animals grow and change until they become adults. When they are adults, they are able to **mate**. To mate is to join together to make babies.

Mammals are born

7 **Mammal** babies grow and develop inside the bodies of their mothers. Once the babies are born, mammal mothers take care of them. Mammal mothers make milk inside their bodies. The babies drink the milk. Drinking the mother's milk is called **nursing**. Nursing gives babies food they need to grow and develop.

Birds lay eggs

8 Many **birds** mate in the spring. Soon after mating, female birds lay eggs. Adult birds sit on their eggs to keep the embryos inside them warm.

Let me out!

9 When the embryo has grown enough, it hatches from its egg. A baby bird that has just hatched is called a hatchling. The hatchling opens its mouth wide to tell it's parents that it wants to be fed. Its parents bring it food. The hatchling grows quickly. Soon it will be an adult that can make babies of its own. Female birds then lay eggs.

More changes

10 An adult animal is in the last stage of its life cycle. For some animals, the adult stage lasts only a few days. For other animals, the adult stage lasts many years. Adult animals that live for many years may go through more changes as they get older. They may lose their teeth or may not be able to move as quickly as they did when they were younger. An animal dies when it's body stops working. The length of time an animal is expected to live is called its **lifespan**.

Now that you've read the text, go back and see if you can answer your pre-reading questions. Use the T-chart that follows to log your notes.

1. What is the main idea of the text?
2. What information is the author providing me?
3. Why is the author giving me this information?

Chapter 3: Research Simulation Task

Text Sample #1 Plant Life Cycles	Text Sample #2 Animal Life Cycles

• The pattern is:
  1. Seed grows
  2. Makes new seeds
  3. Dies
• Most plants grow the same way
• A plant's life starts with a seed
• Some plants grow fast others grow slow
• Most seeds grow under the ground
• Plants grow up and down. The roots go down and the stem and leaves go up
• Roots help the plant stay in the ground
• Plants need food
• Plants can make their own food
• The stem carries food to the plant
• A flower's job is to make a seed	

Take a look at the T-chart on page 53 that you used to jot down notes. What types of information did you write down as you read? Are any of your thoughts similar to the ones below?

- Animals change as they grow.

- Different animals have different life cycles.

- Animals are born or hatch.

- When animals start to grow before they are born, they are called embryos.

- Parents give baby animals food.

- Animals are alive for different lengths of time.

- Animals change as they get older.

- Animals die when their bodies stop working.

Teacher's Note

Because the PARCC® assessments emphasize nonfiction texts, be sure to give students many opportunities to practice reading informational texts during class. The more nonfiction texts that students read, the more comfortable they will be working with texts and finding important information. Being able to locate important information is an essential part of good research. Identifying and locating the information efficiently is essential in timed tasks.

Types of Questions on the Research Simulation Task (RST)

Now that you have had the chance to practice reading informational texts, we are going to begin to look at the different types of questions that may appear on the Research Simulation Task.

When completing the RST, you will be asked to complete three types of questions:

1. Evidence-Based Selected Response (EBSR)
2. Technology-Enhanced Constructed Response (TECR)
3. Prose-Constructed Responses (PCR)

Let's quickly review basic information about each type of test item.

Evidence-Based Selected Response (EBSR)—An EBSR is a multiple-choice question. All EBSR items are two-part items. The first part tests reading comprehension, and the second part tests the reader's ability to find evidence to support the answer to the first question.

Chapter 3: Research Simulation Task

Technology-Enhanced Constructed Response (TECR)—These test items require that the student highlight text or drag and drop responses into place. Students may be asked to compare and contrast information, select multiple pieces of evidence to support an idea, or select multiple answers that could be considered correct.

Prose-Constructed Response (PCR)—This is the essay. On the RST, the essay usually requires that the reader synthesize information from multiple sources to support an idea. Often the reader is asked to compare and contrast information gathered from the sources.

Practice: Evidence-Based Selected Response (EBSR)

We will begin our RST practice by looking at the Evidence-Based Selected Response items. Most times, the EBSR will ask you to either find the meaning of word, find the section of an article that information can be found, or explain why something happens or happened. Part A asks you to identify the correct meaning or answer, and Part B asks you to support your answer with evidence from the text.

For our example, we will look back at the beginning of the first text that we read "Plant Life Cycles" by Anita Ganeri.

EBSR Example

Nature's Patterns

1 Nature is always changing. Many of the changes that happen follow a **pattern**. This means that they happen over and over again.

2 Plant life cycles follow a pattern. A **seed** grows, makes more seeds, and finally dies. Then the new seeds grow and make their own seeds. The cycle starts again.

New Plants

3 There are many different kinds of plants. But most of them will grow in the same way. Most new plants have a life cycle that starts with a **seed**.

4 New plants **sprout** from seeds. Some plants grow very quickly. Other plants grow slowly. Trees are plants that can take many years to grow to their full size.

Growing Seeds

5 Most **seeds** grow in soil. They start to grow into plants under the soil. When a seed starts to grow, this is called **germination**.

6 First, the hard case around the seed breaks open. Then, a root grows down into the soil. A first shoot grows up and the plant's first leaves begin to open.

 **Questions**

1. **Part A**

    What is meaning of the word **sprout** as used in paragraph 4?

    Ⓐ to plant

    Ⓑ to die

    Ⓒ to grow

    Ⓓ to feed

    Part B

    What phrase from the text helps the reader understand the meaning of the word **sprout**?

    Ⓐ ". . . starts with a seed" (paragraph 3)

    Ⓑ ". . . grow very quickly" (paragraph 4)

    Ⓒ "Trees are plants . . ." (paragraph 4)

    Ⓓ "New Plants . . ." (paragraph 4)

    The correct answer for Part A is C: "to grow."

    The correct answer for PART B is B: ". . . grow very quickly (paragraph 4)."

In this context, "sprout" means "to grow." You will see the word "grow" repeated in each sentence in the paragraph. The words around the word you are asked to define will often help you grasp the meaning.

EBSR Practice #1

Now, try answering the question set below on your own.

2. Part A

What is the meaning of the word pattern as used in paragraph 1?

- Ⓐ Something that changes
- Ⓑ Something that is new
- Ⓒ Something that repeats
- Ⓓ Something that dies

Part B

What phrase from the text helps the reader understand the meaning of the word pattern?

- Ⓐ "... happen over and over again." (paragraph 1)
- Ⓑ "... always changing." (paragraph 1)
- Ⓒ "Many of the changes ..." (paragraph 1)
- Ⓓ "Plant life cycles ..." (paragraph 2)

The correct answer to Part A is C: "something that repeats."

The correct answer to Part B is A: " ... happen over and over again (paragraph 1)."

EBSR Practice #2

Now that you are familiar with the structure of the EBSR items, let's look back at the text "Animal Life Cycles—Growing and Changing" that you read in Informational Text Sample #2, and answer the EBSR items that follow.

Animal Life Cycles—Growing and Changing

By Bobbie Kalman

Animal life cycles

1 Animals are living things. Living things breathe, eat, grow, and change. There are many kinds of animals. Some are tiny, and others are huge! As animals grow, they go through many stages, or sets of changes. The stages that animals go through make up their life cycles. Different animals have different life cycles.

Changing animals

2 Animals are born or hatch from eggs. The animals then grow and change into adults. Adult animals are fully grown and can make babies of their own.

Growing embryos

3 When animals begin to grow, they are called embryos. Some embryos grow inside the bodies of their mothers. Other embryos grow inside eggs that are laid by their mothers.

Some animals are born

4 Animal mothers that have embryos growing inside their bodies are pregnant. When an embryo has finished growing, it is born. It leaves its mother's body.

Breaking Out

5 Embryos that do not grow inside the bodies of their mothers grow inside eggs that were laid by their mothers. When the embryos have grown enough, they **hatch**. To hatch is to break out of an egg. Babies that hatch from eggs are called hatchlings.

Growing up

6 Young animals grow and change until they become adults. When they are adults, they are able to mate. To mate is to join together to make babies.

Mammals are born

7 **Mammal** babies grow and develop inside the bodies of their mothers. Once the babies are born, mammal mothers take care of them. Mammal mothers make milk inside their bodies. The babies drink the milk. Drinking the mother's milk is called **nursing**. Nursing gives babies food they need to grow and develop.

Birds lay eggs

8 Many birds mate in the spring. Soon after mating, female birds lay eggs. Adult birds sit on their eggs to keep the embryos inside them warm.

Let me out!

9 When the embryo has grown enough, it hatches from its egg. A baby bird that has just hatched is called a hatchling. The hatchling opens its mouth wide to tell its parents that it wants to be fed. Its parents bring it food. The hatchling grows quickly. Soon it will be an adult that can make babies of its own. Female birds then lay eggs.

More changes

10 An adult animal is in the last stage of its life cycle. For some animals, the adult stage lasts only a few days. For other animals, the adult stage lasts many years. Adult animals that live for many years may go through more changes as they get older. They may lose their teeth or may not be able to move as quickly as they did when they were younger. An animal dies when its body stops working. The length of time an animal is expected to live is called its lifespan.

Questions

1. Part A

   What is the meaning of the word embryo as used in paragraph 3?

   Ⓐ food for an animal

   Ⓑ an adult animal

   Ⓒ an egg

   Ⓓ an unborn animal

Part B
What phrase from the text helps the reader understand the meaning of the word **embryo**?

- Ⓐ "... grow inside eggs ..." (paragraph 3)
- Ⓑ "... inside the bodies ..." (paragraph 3)
- Ⓒ "... by their mothers (paragraph 3)
- Ⓓ "Leaves its mother's body ..." (paragraph 4)

Correct Answers (Part A: D. Part B: D.)

2. Part A
What is the meaning of the word **lifespan** as used in paragraph 10?

- Ⓐ birth
- Ⓑ death
- Ⓒ life expectancy
- Ⓓ life changes

Part B
What phrase from the text helps the reader understand the meaning of the word **lifespan**?

- Ⓐ "... body stops working." (paragraph 10)
- Ⓑ "... time an animal is expected" (paragraph 10)
- Ⓒ "... they were younger" (paragraph 10)
- Ⓓ "... live for many years ..." (paragraph 10)

Correct answers (Part A: C. Part B: B.)

3. Part A

What section from "Animal Life Cycles" explains the physical changes an animal goes through as an adult?

- Ⓐ Growing Embryos
- Ⓑ Breaking Out
- Ⓒ Let me out!
- Ⓓ More changes

Part B

What statement from the article best supports the answer for Part A?

- Ⓐ An adult animal is the last stage of its lifecycle.
- Ⓑ They may lose their teeth or may not be able to move as quickly as they did when they were younger.
- Ⓒ The hatchling opens its mouth wide to tell its parents that it wants to be fed.
- Ⓓ Young animals grow and change until they become adults.

Correct Answers (Part A: D., Part B: B.)

EBSR Practice #3

Read the following excerpts and answer the EBSR items that follow.

The Rise of Machu Picchu

By Kristin B. Rattini

1 Machu Picchu was constructed some 500 years ago during the Inca Empire. This powerful civilization thrived during the 15th and 16th centuries, ruling parts of western South America. Archaeologists believe that it took hundreds of builders to construct the mountaintop city, which was a five day trek from the empire's capital. Using stones from an on-site quarry, they made houses, temples, and even fountains. They also built more than one hundred stone staircases to connect different levels in and around the city. After the Inca Empire fell in the middle 1500s, Machu Picchu was abandoned.

2 Few knew about the neglected metropolis until an American explorer stumbled upon its ruins in July 1911. As news of his discovery spread around the world, so did theories about the mysterious sky high city. Many people thought Machu Picchu was a fortress where the Inca battled invaders. Some have even suggested that aliens built it to have a base on planet Earth. (Yeah, not likely.) Recently scientists digging for clues about the purpose of Machu Picchu have made some interesting finds.

 **Questions**

1. **Part A**
   What is the meaning of the word **theories** as used in paragraph 2?

   Ⓐ an idea that might explain something

   Ⓑ evidence

   Ⓒ a fact about something

   Ⓓ details

   Part B
   What phrase from the text helps the reader understand the meaning of the word **theories**?

   Ⓐ "Many people thought" (paragraph 2)

   Ⓑ "As news of his discovery . . ." (paragraph 2)

   Ⓒ ". . . mysterious sky high city." (paragraph 2)

   Ⓓ ". . . Machu Picchu was a fortress . . ." (paragraph 2)

Correct Answers (Part A: A. Part B: A.)

Chapter 3: Research Simulation Task 67

2. Part A
What best explains why the purpose of Machu Picchu was a mystery?

Ⓐ Machu Picchu was constructed high on a mountaintop.

Ⓑ Machu Picchu was a secure fortress.

Ⓒ Machu Picchu was abandoned for hundreds of years.

Ⓓ Machu Picchu was in South America.

Part B
What sentence best supports the answer for Part A?

Ⓐ Few knew about the neglected city until an American Explorer stumbled upon its ruins in July 1911.

Ⓑ Using stones from an on-site quarry, they made houses, temples, and even fountains.

Ⓒ This powerful city thrived during the 15th and 16th centuries.

Ⓓ They also built more than one hundred stone staircases to connect different levels in and around the city.

Correct Answers (Part A: C. Part B: A.)

EBSR Practice #4

Read the following excerpt and answer the EBSR items that follow.

The Secrets of Stonehenge

By Kristin B. Rattini

1 For centuries people have tried to unlock Stonehenge's secrets. A legend from the 12th century claimed that giants placed the monument on a mountain in Ireland, then a wizard named Merlin magically moved the stone circle to England.

2 Other theories have suggested that migrants from continental Europe built the site as an astronomical observatory or as a temple to the sun and moon gods. No theories have been proven. But a new find may provide more information about the builders of Stonehenge and could help explain why the monument was constructed in this region.

3 Many scientists had guessed that the builders of Stonehenge were the first to settle the area some 5,000 years ago around 3000 B.C. when construction on the site began. A recent excavation is making people rethink this idea.

4 While digging around a spring about a mile and a half from Stonehenge, archaeologist David Jacques and his team uncovered hundreds of bones belonging to aurochs—a species of cattle twice the size of a modern day bull. That suggests that the spring was a pit stop along an auroch migration route where the animals drank water.

5 The team also unearthed 31,000 flints, a stone tool used for hunting. "We started to wonder if the area was also a hunting ground and feasting site for ancient people," Jacques says. "Just one auroch could've fed a hundred people, so the place would've been a big draw." One of the excavated flints was made from a type of rock found some 75 miles to the west. "This means people may have traveled from all over to hunt here," Jacques says.

 **Questions**

1. Part A

What is the meaning of the word excavation as used in paragraph 3?

Ⓐ an idea

Ⓑ construction

Ⓒ dig

Ⓓ journey

Part B

What phrase from the text helps the reader understand the meaning of the word excavation?

Ⓐ "... is making people rethink ..." (paragraph 3)

Ⓑ "Many scientists had guessed ..." (paragraph 3)

Ⓒ "... first to settle ..." (paragraph 3)

Ⓓ "... uncovered hundreds of bones ..." (paragraph 4)

Correct Answers (Part A: C. Part B: D.)

Chapter 3: Research Simulation Task

2. Part A

What best explains that ancient people traveled long distances to the sight of Stonehenge?

- Ⓐ It was a hunting ground that provided large amounts of food.
- Ⓑ The rock formation was very interesting.
- Ⓒ It was created by a wizard.
- Ⓓ It provided shelter during long winters.

Part B

What sentence best supports the answer for Part A?

- Ⓐ The team unearthed 31,000 flints, a stone tool used for hunting.
- Ⓑ One of the excavated flints was made from a type of rock found some 75 miles to the west.
- Ⓒ That suggests that the spring was a pit stop along an auroch migration route where the animals drank water.
- Ⓓ Many scientists had guessed that the builders of Stonehenge were the first to settle the area some 5,000 years ago, around 3000 B.C.

Correct Answers (Part A: A. Part B: B.)

Technology-Enhanced Constructed Response (TECR)

Now, let's move on to work on Technology-Enhanced Constructed Response (TECR) items that will be included in the Research Simulation Task portion of the PARCC test. As noted earlier, these items will require that you manipulate text by highlighting or use a drag-and-drop action. Many of the TECR items ask that you sort information, select multiple pieces of evidence to support a response, or compare and contrast information.

In the following section, you will have an opportunity to practice some of the skills that are assessed on TECR items.

For our first TECR practice item, we will take a look back at "Plant Life Cycles" by Anita Ganeri and "Animal Life Cycles—Growing and Changing" by Bobbie Kalman. Earlier, we recommended that you actively engage in reading and record your thoughts and important information using a T-chart. An example T-chart follows on the next page. When testing, you may need to refer back to the texts, but you will find the T-chart useful when answering some of the TECR items.

TECR Practice #1

Plants and animals have life cycles with both similarities and differences. Compare and contrast the life cycles of plants and animals. Read the phrases below and drag and drop them into the Venn Diagram. (Here, write the phrases where they belong in the diagram.) All phrases will be used. If you do not understand how to use a Venn Diagram, be sure to ask your teacher to explain before you begin.

- Require food to grow
- Have different life cycles
- Make new life
- Nurse their young

- Can grow large or small
- Grow the same way
- Feed themselves

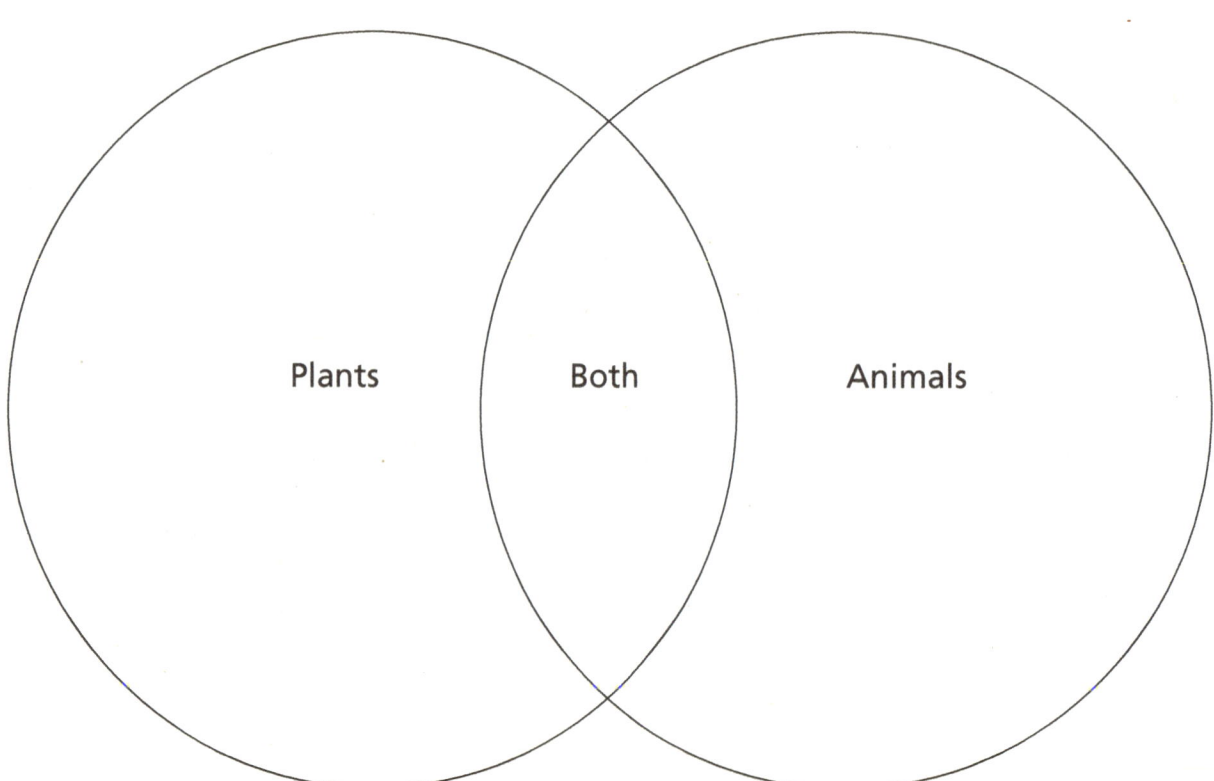

Chapter 3: Research Simulation Task

TECR Practice #2

You have read about the plant life cycle. Place the following phases from a plant's life cycle in the order that they occur. (You can rewrite the list here.)

- The hard shell of the seed breaks open.

- A shoot grows up from the ground.

- A root grows down into the soil.

- A seed germinates.

- Plant leaves collect sunlight.

_____

_____

_____

_____

TECR Practice #3

Drag and drop the event from of the animal life cycle that closely matches the plant life cycle event. (Here, write the sentence in the empty boxes in the chart.)

- An animal's teeth fall out.

- A hatchling breaks open an egg.

- A mammal nurses its baby.

Plant Life Cycle Event	Animal Life Cycle Event
The stem comes up through the soil.	
A petal drops from a flower.	
A root soaks up nutrients from the soil.	

Prose-Constructed Response (PCR)

On the PARCC®, the Prose-Constructed Response (PCR) item is the essay. You will analyze the information that you have read, and put it together to write a response. It is important that you use evidence directly from the text to support the ideas that you express in your writing. You will be expected to apply your knowledge of language and writing conventions when completing the essay. In order to successfully complete the task, you should also be able to take brief notes and sort information.

The obvious challenge for you will be to construct a response on the computer. You may not have had much experience typing essays, and much of the experience that you do have is probably limited to typing the final draft of an essay that was written using pencil and paper. To make constructing an essay online as easy as possible, it is important to keep information easy to access and organized. Remember: Simplicity is key when you need to organize your thoughts!

You might feel in a rush to write the essay question. You might be tempted to just rewrite the text, but if you do, you'll end up writing a summary of the texts rather than a response base on evidence. To avoid this, slow down and take the time to think before you write. If you take the time to read the question carefully and take a minute to think about your response, success will follow.

During our practice assignment, you will get a chance to practice reading some more informational texts. Be sure to take notes and organize important information using a T-chart.

When writing the essay, you should take the following steps:

Before Writing:

1. Read the question carefully. Make sure you understand what you need to write about.
2. Take a look back at the notes that you took as you read.
3. Compare and contrast the information you gathered and see if you can find a connection between the information from the two sources.

Chapter 3: Research Simulation Task

When Writing:

4. Make sure to use a topic sentence that answers the question in the PCR item prompt.
5. Make sure to include supporting details from both/all sources.
6. Refer back to the article when selecting evidence from the text.

After Writing:

7. Reread your response to make sure ideas were expressed clearly
8. Proofread your response for punctuation and grammar.

Practice: Prose-Constructed Response (PCR)

Today, you will do some research on underwater animals. First, you will read an article "Ooh! . . . Orcas!" Then, you will read the article "Everyone Wants to Know About Sharks." As you read these sources, you will gather information and answer questions so you can write a response.

Ooh ... Orcas!

By Kathy Kranking

It's easy to recognize **orcas**—they're dressed like giant Oreo cookies! But that's not all that's cool about them. There's more: they breathe from the tops of their heads. They can "see" with sound. And they're actually giant dolphins!

Orcas' size and strength are two other amazing things about these animals. An orca looks like a black-and-white torpedo bursting from the water. A large male orca is almost as long as a school bus, and it weighs more than 10 bottle-nose dolphins do!

Orcas are powerful swimmers, too. They can reach speeds of more than 35 miles per hour in short bursts—and that's super fast for moving through water!

Blending in

Orcas are the largest members of the dolphin family. They live in every ocean of the world, though most of them are found in colder waters along coasts.

Those famous black-and-white markings are more than just pretty: they help with camouflage. When seen from above, the orca's black back blends in with the dark water. This makes it hard for animals looking at the water from an ice floe or beach to spot an orca. From below, an orca's white belly blends with the light coming from above, making it harder for prey animals to see an orca swimming above them.

Hole in the Head

Like other dolphins, an orca breathes through a **blowhole** on the top of its head. When the orca surfaces, it blows air out of the hole to exhale. Then it takes in a big breath before diving under again. To keep water from getting into the blowhole, a special muscle closes it up tight.

Family Ties

Orcas travel in family groups called **pods**. A pod can have as few as five members or as many as forty. Sometimes pods combine to make groups of more than a hundred orcas.

Pods are usually made up of related mother orcas and their male and female young. Orca family bonds are very strong, and members may stay together for life.

Orcas belong to different groups, called **ecotypes**. Scientists have discovered that each orca ecotype has its own behaviors that are different from those of other ecotypes. For example, some ecotypes eat only fish, while others eat only marine mammals. And some are very playful, while others are calmer.

Orca Chat

If you could dive into the water and swim along with a group of orcas, you'd be amazed at the noise you'd hear all around you. That's because orcas "talk" to each other using different sounds.

The three main sounds orcas make are clicks, whistles, and pulsing calls, but they also make popping sounds and jaw claps. They'll even slap their fins and tails against the surface of the water to make loud noises. Some of the sounds can be heard for miles! Scientists are studying orca talk to try to figure out what it all means.

On the Hunt

Orcas are also called "killer whales" because they're such fierce predators. Whether they hunt separately or in a group, they have some clever tricks for catching prey. For example, orcas may swim toward an ice floe with a seal on it to make a big wave that knocks the seal off. Or an orca may come right out of the water onto a beach or an ice floe to grab prey.

A group of orcas will herd a school of fish into a tight circle, and then whack at the group with their tails. This knocks out the fish so that the orcas can more easily gobble them up.

An orca's sharp, cone-shaped teeth are perfect for ripping and tearing food. Depending on their ecotype, orcas eat a variety of prey, including seals, fish, penguins, sea turtles, whales, and even other dolphins.

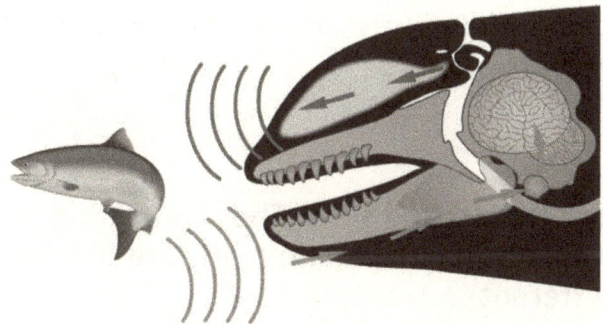

Seeing with Sound

An orca has a neat way of zeroing in on prey: it uses echoes. This is called **echolocation**. Here's how it works: first an orca makes some clicking sounds by passing air between lip-like parts in its head, called **phonic lips**. The sounds pass through another part in the orca's head, called the **melon**. The melon helps aim the sounds straight ahead. If the sounds hit something in front of the orca, they bounce back as echoes. The sounds travel through a fat-filled part of the orca's jaw to its ears, which are inside its head.

By listening to the sounds, the orca can tell the size and shape of the object, as well as how far away it is and which way it's going. Orcas also use echolocation to find their way in murky water. So they really are "seeing" with sound!

Everyone Wants to Know About Sharks

By Kathy Kranking

You probably recognize the **great white shark**, one of the most famous species of all. And you know that, like many other sharks, they're expert predators. But what else do you really know about sharks?

These toothy fish have a reputation for being scary. Even so, there are more than 440 species of sharks, and less than one percent of those species are dangerous to people.

Sharks live in oceans all over the world. Some kinds live close to the surface, some in deeper waters, and some near the ocean floor. No matter what part of the ocean they're found in, sharks have been swimming there for a long time—since way before dinosaurs existed. Scientists have found fossilized shark teeth that are more than 400 million years old.

Assorted Sharks

Sharks come in different shapes and sizes. They can be bigger than a bus or only a little longer than your hand. And though many are the familiar torpedo shape, some can look quite different.

The biggest shark—and the biggest of all fish—is the **whale shark**. Despite its huge size, this gentle giant eats tiny animals called **plankton**. As it swims along with its mouth open, the plankton get swept inside. The water goes back out through the shark's gills, while the plankton continue to the back of the shark's mouth. Then the shark swallows its meal.

Built to Bite

Most sharks, though, hunt down and eat other animals. And they have everything they need to be amazing predators. Take their teeth, for instance. Most toothed animals have just one set of teeth for their whole lives. But sharks have many rows of teeth. As old teeth wear out or break, new ones keep moving up to replace them. A shark may grow thousands of teeth during its lifetime!

The shape of a shark's teeth depends on what kind of prey it catches. Teeth with saw-like edges are used for cutting and tearing large prey such as fish. Long, curved teeth are great for catching slippery prey such as squid. And flat teeth crunch up crabs and other shellfish.

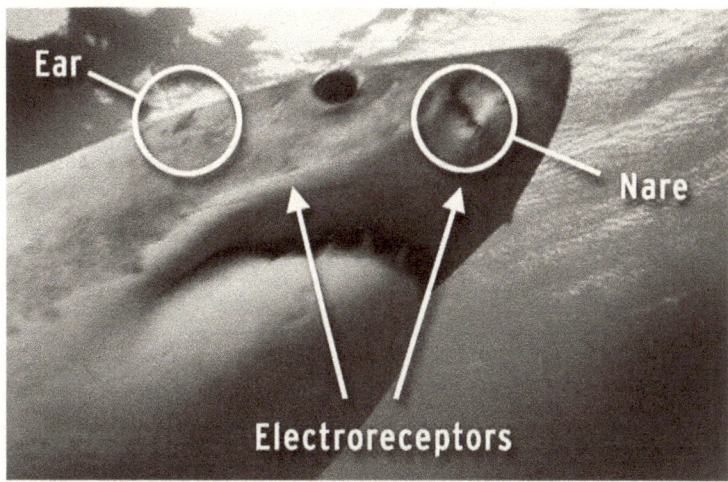

Super Senses

Sharks have excellent senses that help make them great predators. One of the best is their sense of smell. They can smell things that a person never could! Smelling is the only job a shark's nostrils have—sharks do their breathing through gills.

Tiny **pores**, or openings, on a shark's snout help it with another sense. They pick up electrical signals from prey (all living things give off small amounts of electricity).

Like other fish, a shark also has something called a **lateral line** along each side of its body. This is a line of pores that are sensitive to vibrations. A shark can use its lateral line to detect movements of prey.

Prose-Constructed Response Item

Write an essay comparing and contrasting the key details presented in the two articles above, and explain how underwater animals use their senses to survive. Use specific details and examples from both articles to support your ideas.

Practice: Full Research Simulation Task

Now, you will try your hand at a full Research Simulation Task all on your own! First, you will do some research on animal rescues. You will begin your research by reading an article about rescuing a beaver. Then you will read an article about rescuing a bald eagle. As you read these sources, you will gather information and answer questions about animals and their rehabilitation, so that you can write an essay response.

Mission Animal Rescue: Beaver

By Scott Elder

1 The baby beaver paddles furiously, trying to escape the surging river that's sweeping him downstream. A strong current during a storm pulled him away from his lodge on the Bow River in Calgary, Canada, and now the animal is miles from his parents. As rain and wind pummel the waterway, the beaver struggles to stay afloat. Eventually the river calms and the baby swims to shore. Using the last of his strength, he scrambles onto the bank and curls up, exhausted and scared.

Safe at Last

2 After the rain passes, an employee at the concrete company that's located on the river bank arrives for work. At the water's edge he notices the soggy baby beaver, called a kit, balled up on the ground. Realizing that the kit needs help the man scoops him up and drives to a nearby animal hospital. From here the beaver is transported by a volunteer to the Calgary Wildlife Rehabilitation Society, where he will begin his recovery.

3 Vets check the kit—now named Birch—for wounds or broken bones. Fortunately they find no injuries. "But he's a real little guy—only three and a half pounds," says Andrea Hunt, a worker at the rehab center. Based on his weight, staff estimates that Birch is about 8 weeks old. "Baby beavers stay with their families for one to two years," Hunt says. "He's not ready to care for himself. If he hadn't been rescued, he almost certainly wouldn't have survived."

Busy Beavers

4 To keep Birch from getting lonely, the staff paired him with a rescued female baby beaver named Aspen. The kits are eventually moved into two neighboring enclosures each measuring about 19 feet by 13 feet. At first they're fed a milky cereal that they lap up from bowls. A few weeks later, Birch and Aspen begin a diet of solid food that includes leafy kale and collard greens. Also on the menu is beavers' signature snack: wood. Volunteers bring stacks of freshly cut tree branchs, which the kits hungrily **gnaw** at to get to the tasty inner bark.

5 For exercise, each beaver receives its own inflatable kiddie pool to swim in. "But beavers have an instinct to chomp on things," Hunt says. "After about a day, they chew up all the plastic." Their replacement pools—four-foot-wide circular troughs—are made of beaver proof steel. Staff also increase the animals' wood supply so they have plenty of healthy wood to gnaw on.

6 Over time the beavers begin to stack uneaten branches left in their enclosures. "Beavers are known for their ability to build sturdy homes by piling sticks and mud," Hunt says. "Birch and Aspen seem to be taking a swing at constructing beaver lodges." The caretakers are thrilled to see the animals exhibiting wild beaver behavior.

Homeward Bound

7 About a year after his rescue, Birch weighs in at a robust 27 pounds. "Not only is he healthy but he is showing good survival skills," Hunt says. "It's time we let him go." Early one morning the beaver is driven to a Canadian forest to be released. Aspen will be let go later in the week so she remains behind at the center. At the release site, Birch is carried in a cage to the bank of a lake. When the door opens, he cautiously steps out, then slips into the water and paddles away. "We'll miss Birch," Hunt says. "But nothing feels better than putting an animal back where it belongs."

 **Questions**

Evidence-Based Selected Response Items

1. Part A
What is meaning of the word **gnaw** as it is used in paragraph 4?

Ⓐ hit

Ⓑ break

Ⓒ chew

Ⓓ break

Part B

What phrase from the text helps the reader understand the meaning of the word gnaw?

- Ⓐ ". . . moved into two neighboring enclosures" (paragraph 3)
- Ⓑ ". . . freshly cut tree branches . . ." (paragraph 4)
- Ⓒ "Volunteers bring snacks . . ." (paragraph 4)
- Ⓓ ". . . the kits hungrily" (paragraph 4)

Correct Answers (Part A: C. Part B: A.)

2. Part A

What section from "Mission Animal Rescue: Beaver" explains that the beaver is ready to be released into its natural habitat?

- Ⓐ Busy Beavers
- Ⓑ Homeward Bound
- Ⓒ Safe at Last
- Ⓓ Chow Time

Part B

What statement from the article best supports the answer for Part A?

- Ⓐ "Not only is he healthy but he has also shown good survival skills."
- Ⓑ "Birch is carried in a cage to the end of a lake."
- Ⓒ "To keep Birch from getting lonely, staff pair him with a rescued female baby Beaver named Aspen."
- Ⓓ "Vets check the kit—now named Birch—for wounds or broken bones."

Correct Answers (Part A: B. Part B: A.)

3. Part A

What is the main idea of Mission Animal Rescue: Beaver?

Ⓐ It is important to remove beavers from the wild because they can be destructive.

Ⓑ A beaver is a dangerous animal if not trained properly.

Ⓒ Beavers use wood as a resource for survival.

Ⓓ A young beaver gets help from caring people.

Part B

What statement from the article best supports the answer for Part A?

Ⓐ "But beavers have an instinct to chomp on things."

Ⓑ "If he hadn't been rescued, he almost certainly wouldn't have survived."

Ⓒ "After about a day, they chew up all the plastic."

Ⓓ "Beavers are known for their ability to build sturdy homes by piling sticks and mud."

Correct Answers (Part A: D. Part B: B.)

Technology-Enhanced Constructed Response Items

Highlight two sentences in the article that show how humans helped the beaver.

Mission Animal Rescue: Bald Eagle

By Kitson Jazynka

1 A bald eagle lies in the gravel along a busy highway near Spokane, Washington. Her feathers ruffle in the breeze. The majestic bird's body is limp, and her wings droop at her sides. She's accidentally ingested pesticide—poison used by farmers to protect their harvests from crop-destroying pests. Too weak to stay aloft in the air, the bird crash-landed on the roadside and can now barely move. Without help, she won't make it.

On the Mend

2 A driver traveling down the highway spots the large bird and pulls over. Seeing that the eagle is still breathing, the driver wraps her in a blanket and rushes to Mount Spokane Veterinary Hospital. Here veterinarian Pearce Fujiura gives the nine-pound, five-year-old bird a checkup. X-rays show that she has no broken bones. "But otherwise it's not looking good," Fujiura says. The bird can't lift her head or flap her wings. And she's so skinny that Fujiura can see the outline of her keel, or breastbone, under her feathers.

3 Based on the eagle's condition, the vet suspects that she's eaten poison. So he pumps charcoal through a tube down the bird's beak and into her digestive tract. An absorbent material, the charcoal will soak up the toxins in her body. Then Fujiura settles the bird, now named Glenda, in a comfy three-by-three-foot cage and leaves her to rest.

4 The next morning Fujiura finds Glenda standing in her cage. Eyeing the vet, the eagle opens her beak, fluffs her feathers, and raises a talon. It's a good sign. "She's already stronger and more alert," Fujiura says. He moves Glenda to a 16-by-12-foot outdoor enclosure where she'll have more room to move around and offers her a large dead rat as a meal. The hungry bird devours the snack. Over the next few days the staff at the animal hospital keep a close eye on the still-fragile eagle, giving her fresh-caught trout and salmon to eat. Under their care, Glenda continues to improve.

Takeoff Trouble

5 A month later Glenda weighs a little over 11 pounds and is much more active. She likes to perch on the side of her water tub, jump in, and splash around.

6 The bird also tries to fly, hopping on the logs in her enclosure and spreading her wings for takeoff. But she can only rise a few feet before having to land. "Her right wing hangs a bit lower than it should," Fujiura says. "We realize she might have an injury that our x-ray machine didn't pick up." This is bad news—if Glenda can't fly, she won't survive in the wild.

7 Fujiura decides to transfer the bird to Washington State University's College of Veterinary Medicine in Pullman, Washington. The college has a larger care center for birds and stronger x-ray machines that can reveal what's wrong with Glenda's wing. After loading the eagle into a dog crate, Fujiura drives her the two hours to Pullman.

8 At the college, veterinarian Nickol Finch takes x-rays of the bird and discovers a tiny fracture close to Glenda's elbow. Although it's almost healed, the doctors still aren't sure whether she'll be able to take flight. "It can be hard for birds to relearn how to use a wing that's been injured, even after it's better," Fujiura says. "We just have to wait and see." The animal is placed with other eagles at the college in a huge 20-by-120 foot special bird enclosure called an aviary. After two months Glenda begins to fly again.

Volunteers carefully release a bald eagle into the wild.

Independence Day

9 The staff helps Glenda improve her soaring skills by placing food high up in the aviary, motivating her to fly up to the chow. By November she's ready to be released. The eagle is placed in a crate and driven by Fujiura and Finch to a nearby state park. When Finch opens the crate by a hillside, Glenda steps out and flies up into a tree. After basking in the sun, the eagle spreads her wings and soars out of sight. "Glenda has such a strong will to survive," Fujiura says. "It's thrilling to see her free once again."

 **Questions**

Evidence-Based Selected Response Item #1

1. Part A

What is the meaning of the word **absorbent** as it is used in paragraph 3?

- Ⓐ soft
- Ⓑ hard
- Ⓒ spongy
- Ⓓ shiny

Part B

What phrase from the text helps the reader understand the meaning of the word absorbent?

Ⓐ So he pumps charcoal . . ." (paragraph 3)

Ⓑ ". . . the charcoal will soak up . . ." (paragraph 3)

Ⓒ ". . . in a comfy three-by-three foot cage . . ." (paragraph 3)

Ⓓ ". . . through a tube . . ." (paragraph 3)

Correct Answers (Part A: C. Part B: B.)

2. Part A

What is the main idea of "Mission: Animal Rescue Bald Eagle"?

Ⓐ Bald Eagles are a patriotic symbol and should be rescued.

Ⓑ Eagles cannot fly unless they are taught to fly.

Ⓒ Dedicated volunteers help an injured eagle fly again.

Ⓓ Training a bald eagle can be very challenging.

Part B

What statement from the article best supports the answer for Part A?

Ⓐ Over the next few days staff at the animal hospital keep a close eye on the still fragile eagle.

Ⓑ Based on the eagle's condition, the vet suspects that she's eaten poison.

Ⓒ The majestic bird's body is limp, and her wings droop at her sides.

Ⓓ This is bad news—if Glenda can't fly, she won't survive in the wild.

Correct Answers (Part A: C. Part B: A.)

Chapter 3: Research Simulation Task

Evidence-Based Selected Response Item #2

Select the statements below that describe both the rescue of the beaver and the rescue of the bald eagle. Select all that apply.

Ⓐ Veterinarians assisted with the rescue.

Ⓑ The animals were released into the wild within days.

Ⓒ The animals were badly injured.

Ⓓ After they were rehabilitated, the animals were released into the wild.

Ⓔ The animals were fed salmon and trout.

Correct Answers (A, D)

Prose-Constructed Response

You have read the articles "Mission Animal Rescue: Beaver" and "Mission Animal Rescue: Bald Eagle." Think about the key details in each article that explain why animals are rescued and show how people help animals return to their natural habitats.

Write an essay comparing and contrasting the key details presented in the two articles, and explain why animals need to be rescued and how humans help injured animals return to the wild. Use specific details and examples from both articles to support your ideas.

You can use the PARCC® Literary Analysis and Research Rubric in Appendix B in the back of this book to see just how well you have done!

CHAPTER 4

Narrative Task

Task Time: 90 minutes

A Message to Educators and Parents

The PARCC® Narrative Task may appear deceptively easy at first glance. Some educators and parents may think that since most third graders know the parts of a narrative and how to write a simple story, this task should be pretty easy, but this task asks more of students than simply writing a story. Students first have to analyze a story or excerpt through the multiple-choice questions, and then write their own story *based on that analysis*. It is this last evidence-based step that can trip students up.

To be successful in this task on the PARCC® exam, students must not only be able to identify key story elements and character traits, but also *analyze* the narrative, then use their imaginations in tandem with instructions in a prompt, to write an essay that augments the story. For example, students may be asked to write a journal entry about what they imagine a particular character in the reading is experiencing, or they may be asked to write their own ending to a given story. They will not be writing a spontaneous random story of their own.

The more practice students have in narrative writing, coupled with analysis and response to a prompt, the better they will do on the exam. This task is well within the reach of most third graders, but they will feel much more comfortable with the task on the PARCC® test if they have first worked through the practice session in this chapter and the practice test later in the book.

This chapter is aligned with the following Common Core standards:

CCSS.ELA-Literacy.RL.3.1	CCSS.ELA-Literacy.L.3.1
CCSS.ELA-Literacy.RL.3.2	CCSS.ELA-Literacy.L.3.2
CCSS.ELA-Literacy.RL.3.3	CCSS.ELA-Literacy.L.3.3
CCSS.ELA-Literacy.RL.3.4	CCSS.ELA-Literacy.L.3.4
CCSS.ELA-Literacy.RL.3.5	CCSS.ELA-Literacy.L.3.5
CCSS.ELA-Literacy.RL.3.6	CCSS.ELA-Literacy.W.3.1
CCSS.ELA-Literacy.RL.3.7	CCSS.ELA-Literacy.W.3.2
CCSS.ELA-Literacy.RL.3.8	CCSS.ELA-Literacy.W.3.3
CCSS.ELA-Literacy.RL.3.9	CCSS.ELA-Literacy.W.3.4
CCSS.ELA-Literacy.RL.3.10	CCSS.ELA-Literacy.W.3.5
CCSS.ELA-Literacy.RF.3.4	CCSS.ELA-Literacy.W.3.6

Introduction

As we discussed in the Introduction chapter of this book, organization and attention to detail are very important when reading and writing.

The practice Narrative Task that follows is very similar to what you will find on the PARCC® test, which will include a reading, multiple-choice questions, and a narrative writing assignment. Here is what you will do in the Practice Session that follows:

1. **Narrative Reading.** You will read a short story and answer the multiple-choice questions that follow. The questions will be connected to both the details and the main ideas of the reading.

2. **Narrative Writing Exercise #1**. Write a journal entry about how you imagine the experiences of one of the characters in the story, including information about how this character responded to the events in the story. You will need to use your imagination to add details of the character's feelings, thoughts, and actions to those already included in the story.

3. **Pre-writing.** Fill out a Pre-writing Graphic Organizer in which you divide the story into a beginning, middle, and end. As you fill out this graphic organizer, you will tell the story as you imagine the one character experienced it. You will want to make sure your thoughts are organized, and that your writing includes traits of that character from the story. You will need to use your imagination to think up what more that character might have been feeling and doing during the story!

Chapter 4: Narrative Task

4. **Narrative Writing #2.** You will rewrite your journal entry, using the beginning, middle, and end that you wrote in the Pre-writing Graphic Organizer.

You will need to refer to the PARCC® Prose-Constructed Response Narrative Rubric as you prepare your written responses. You can find this rubric in Appendix B at the end of this test prep book. This rubric gives you a summary of the accomplishments that are expected in your writing. You may want to ask your teacher to help you understand the rubric.

Evaluating the Narrative Task

A good practice for the Narrative Task section of the test is to look at the writing prompt *before* you begin reading the narrative excerpt that is included. That way, you can think about what to include in your essay as you read through the excerpt.

Think about how you will work with each task in the essay prompt, and then study the rubric in Appendix B at the back of this book.

Keep in mind the beginning, middle, and ending of a short story, as shown in the following diagram. Remember to look at the details given to you in the essay prompt, and to continue the story as directed by the question's instructions. We will review this diagram as we look at a sample response.

This type of organizer, called a Story Pyramid, will help assist you in your brainstorming and pre-writing later in this Practice Session. Put notes next to each part of the Story Pyramid. This will help to organize your plans for writing the short story.

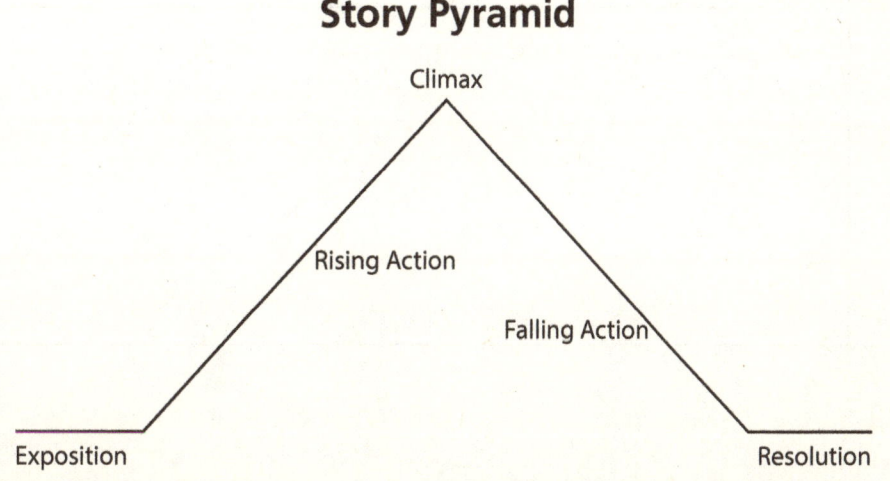

We have put this Story Pyramid into an easy-to-use graphic organizer below. Thinking about the story in chronological order will help speed up your organization of ideas. Because the PARCC® test will be timed, you will want you to organize your thoughts as quickly as possible.

Think about the point at which you are beginning your story—Is the journal entry currently in the rising action? Has the conflict already occurred? Use details from the story that has already been started for you.

Review the graphic organizer below, and then read the story that follows. As you read, think about the story's beginning, middle, and end.

Story Graphic Organizer

Beginning of Story ⬇	
Middle of Story ⬇	
Ending	

Practice: Narrative Task

You are going to start this Practice Session by reading a short story and answering multiple-choice questions about it. Do not worry if you have never read this story before! As you read, take the time to think about the events of the story and the actions of the characters, and you will do fine answering the questions here, and responding to the essay question that follows.

Narrative Reading Exercise

Read the following short story, "Was It a Dream?" by Edith Robarts. Answer the questions that follow, and try to remember the information contained in the questions. It will help you later when you are asked to respond to an essay question about the reading by writing your own narrative story as a journal entry.

Was It a Dream?

By Edith Robarts

1 Rita grew quite tired of gathering wildflowers while her brother, Frank, sat by the water busy with his fishing-rod.

2 "He must be tired of it by this time! He has been fishing for two hours!" she said, and, swinging her bunch of flowers, she walked to where her brother was sitting.

3 "Do leave off fishing for a while, Frank!" she pleaded, leaning against the tree beside him. "There is such a funny-looking animal running about over there in the grass. Come and look!"

4 Frank laughed.

5 "I know your funny-looking animals, Rita!" he said.

6 "Aren't you really tired of sitting quite still?" went on Rita wonderingly.

7 "I don't think about it," answered her brother. "I want to catch the fish, and to do that I must sit still."

FISHING.

8 Rita knew she must be contented to wait, so she walked a little way from him and threw herself down upon the bank.

9 As she lay looking into the water she suddenly felt herself grow very sleepy. A little while after, the water began to get so clear that she could see right through it. It grew more and more so until it became just like glass. Rita could see the very bottom of the pond and the fish swimming quickly backwards and forwards.

10 Then she heard some very funny little voices coming up from the water. This made her look closer, and she soon discovered a small group of fishes who seemed to be speaking very eagerly together. She saw they were gathered round Frank's line, on the end of which hung a tempting piece of bait.

11 "I tell you, my son," Rita heard the largest fish say to one of the smaller ones, "that is a trap. I have seen hundreds of poor fishes try to swallow that worm, and they have been pulled up out of the water and I have never seen them any more!"

12 "But, mother!" cried the smaller fish, "if I only had just one bite! Look what a beauty it is! I am sure there can be nothing to harm me!"

13 "Inside that worm," continued the big fish, "there is a hook which will catch into your gills, and you will not be able to get away. Then the man at the top will pull you up and up, and you will be killed and eaten by him!"

Chapter 4: Narrative Task

14 Still the little fish looked longingly at the bait. Rita wanted to call out and tell him what his mother said was quite true; but somehow her voice refused to come.

15 The other fishes who were gathered round listening did not say anything, but Rita saw that some of the smaller ones looked at the worm just as longingly as the little one who had spoken.

16 For a few minutes there was silence in the water; then all at once, at a moment when it thought its mother was looking the other way, the little fish made a dart forward and tried to swallow the bait. The next moment it was wriggling about in a most pitiable manner and giving faint little cries for help. Its mother swam towards it in great distress.

17 "Come and help!" she called, in a trembling voice.

18 All the other fishes surrounded the line, and some caught hold of the little fish's tail and held on.

19 Just as Rita was getting very excited indeed she gave a great start and jumped up from the bank.

20 "What was that?" she exclaimed aloud.

21 "Why, I've got a splendid catch. It must be a monster! The line is so heavy I can hardly pull it in!"

22 It was Frank's voice. Rita suddenly remembered where she was and that she must have fallen asleep. She walked slowly to Frank, thinking about her strange dream.

23 She had only stood by him a minute when—splash!—out flew the line from the water and over went Frank on his back.

24 It was so funny that Rita could not help laughing heartily—especially as Frank was not at all hurt.

25 "It's all very well for you to laugh!" he said, when he had got up again; "but that was the best catch I've ever had, and the wretched fish must have got off the hook!"

26 Rita grew very thoughtful. Could her dream have been true? It really did seem strange. Anyway, although she felt sorry for Frank, she could not help feeling very pleased that the poor little fish had got free!

Now that you have read through the story, "Was It a Dream?," you will have the opportunity to answer questions related to this reading. Remember that these types of questions are often part-based, which means that your answer to Part A will be directly linked to your answer to Part B.

 **Questions**

1. Part A

Rita wakes up from her dream. How does this affect what happens next in the story?

Ⓐ Rita realizes that she was dreaming, and is confused.

Ⓑ Rita's dream encourages Frank to catch a fish!

Ⓒ Frank becomes a better fisher.

Ⓓ Rita becomes confused as to whether her dream was real or not because her awakened experiences were similar to those of her sleeping experiences.

Part B

Choose two details from the highlighted part of the passage that support the answer to Part A.

Ⓐ ". . . the poor little fish had got free!"

Ⓑ "She had only stood by him a minute when—splash!— "

Ⓒ ". . . and the wretched fish must have got off the hook!"

Ⓓ "Could her dream have been true?"

Ⓔ "It really did seem strange."

Ⓕ "I've got a splendid catch."

Chapter 4: Narrative Task

Below, place the information into the chart the way that Frank responds to each event during his interactions with Rita in the story. Based on your experience with the reading, you have to think about the timing of events. Rita responded very specifically at different times in the reading.

On the PARCC® test, you will be working on a computer screen, so you will be clicking and dragging your responses into the spaces available. In this test prep book, you can just write the responses in the chart instead. Of the five statements, you will be choosing three, so not every response will be used.

2. How Rita Responds:
- Rita laughs.
- Rita moves away onto the grass and falls asleep.
- Rita begins to help her brother, Frank, fish.
- Rita talks to the fish as they swim in the water.
- Rita looks in silence.

Events	How Rita Responds
Frank fished for two hours already.	
The fish begin to talk to one another about the bait.	
Frank falls when trying to catch the fish.	

3. Part A

What is the central message of the story?

Ⓐ Children enjoy fishing.

Ⓑ Animals are extraordinary beings.

Ⓒ Our hobbies can be very important to us.

Ⓓ Many times, our actions can have personal consequences on others.

Part B

Which sentence from the story supports the answer to Part A?

Ⓐ "Its mother swam towards it in great distress."

Ⓑ "All the other fishes surrounded the line."

Ⓒ "For a few minutes there was silence in the water."

Ⓓ ". . . till the little fish looked longingly at the bait."

 **Answer Key**

1. Part A

As you have learned so far, in order to answer this type of question, you must look at Part A first. Answer choices A and D are very similar, but D is more specific to what happens next in the story for Rita.

Part B

Keeping what you've done for Part A in mind, answer choices for Part B can then be chosen! Answers D and E support how Rita was very confused, and was blending her dream with real life by the end of the reading.

2.

Events	How Rita Responds
Frank fished for two hours already.	[Rita moves away onto the grass and falls asleep.]
The fish begin to talk to one another about the bait.	[Rita looks in silence.]
Frank falls when trying to catch the fish.	[Rita laughs.]

3. This part-based question can get a little confusing! When working with Part A, there is no answer that comes to us right away. We do know that Rita, through her dream, realized that Frank's fishing could affect a whole family of fishes. Because of this main point of the story, we would eliminate answer choices A and C because they deal with people, not fishes. This leaves us with selecting between either answer choice B or answer choice D. Going even further, we

Chapter 4: Narrative Task

would select answer choice D because Frank's decision to fish could make significant changes to this fish family we meet in Rita's dream!

In Part B, answer choice A helps the reader understand that Frank's fishing experience could separate and change a family of fish, which Rita may not have realized, were it not for her dream.

Narrative Exercise #1

Now that you have read the story and answered questions about it, it is time to practice the narrative writing part of the Practice Session.

Write a journal entry from Frank about his experiences with fishing in this story, as Rita remains asleep. Include information about how Frank responded to the events in the story as you write your journal entry. You will need to use your imagination here to think up what Frank might have been feeling, thinking, and doing!

_____

_____

_____

_____

_____

_____

_____

_____

Chapter 4: Narrative Task

Pre-writing Exercise

Now that you have completed a journal entry on your own, you are going to write it again—this time by doing some pre-writing first! **Pre-writing** is the thinking and organizing you do before you actually write your narrative. We suggest that you pre-write your journal entry by breaking the narrative into beginning, middle, and end. This will help you organize and rewrite your journal entry in the same way later.

To pre-write, we use our graphic organizer to jot down our thoughts before putting together a model journal entry below that tells how we imagine Frank might be thinking and acting in the beginning, middle, and end of the story.

Prewriting Graphic Organizer

Beginning of Story 	• Frank sees Rita fall asleep on the grass. • As Frank sits patiently fishing, he looks into the water at the beautiful fish.
Middle of Story 	• Frank's mind wanders and he watches the fish surround the bait of his fishing rod. • Frank can hear the fish talking and interacting with one another.
Ending	• Rita wakes up. • Because Frank can overhear the fishes' conversation, he decides to pretend to try to catch the fish in front of Rita, but purposely does not!

Narrative Exercise #2

If this were the real PARCC® test, you would now write your narrative! So to end this Practice Session, write your journal entry again about what Frank experienced in the story. Try including a paragraph on each of the parts of the story (beginning, middle, end). First, read our model response below, and then try writing one by yourself!

Model Journal Entry

I can see Rita falling asleep over there, so I'll sit my fishing pole down and wait for a bite. It's very beautiful outside, as the sky begins to glitter with its bright sun. I could not be happier! I think that fishing is my favorite thing to do! The clear water shows me five fish surrounding the worm that I purchased for bait. I can't believe it! Five fish!

All of a sudden, I hear two fish speaking to each other, like people! Wow! I cannot say anything because I am in shock. One fish has bright blue eyes, and the other had yellow. I learned about fish in my science class last week, but seeing them so clearly is very exciting for me. One fish is larger than the others, and she talks to the four other fish, as if they are her children, just like my own mom! I cannot believe it! The mama fish asks her children nicely not to bite at the worm, but it is dangerous. This is like how my mom gives me advice. Sometimes I listen to mom's advice, and sometimes I don't . . .

I can feel one fish biting at the bait, so I grab the fishing pole and hold on for dear life. It is a battle back and forth, as the fishing line stretches very hard. Rita wakes up and walks over to me, as she looks a little confused! The sun is shining onto my face and I stare into the water. I remember the mama fish and her words, so I let go, and pretend to fall down so Rita believes that I didn't give up on that catch! I'm glad the baby fish got away, and I hope he knows how lucky he is to have a mama who gives good advice!

_____

_____

_____

_____

CHAPTER 5

Practice Tests 1 and 2

In this chapter, you will have the opportunity to work through two complete practice tests, each one similar to the PARCC® English Language Arts/Literacy third grade test you will be taking soon. Each practice test here will have all three parts you will find on the PARCC® test: (1) Literary Analysis Task, (2) Research Simulation Task, and (3) Narrative Task. You have just finished preparing for each of these tasks in Chapters 2 through 4 of this test prep book, so you should be all set for these practice tests!

Practice Test 1

Literary Analysis Task

Task Time: 90 minutes

Today you will read two stories, "The Little Spider's First Web" and "The Secret." As you read, think about the actions of the characters and the events of the stories. Then answer the questions, which will help you respond to the essay question that follows.

Read the story "The Little Spider's First Web." Then answer questions 1 through 3.

The Little Spider's First Web
From *Among the Meadow People* by Clara Dillingham Pierson

1 The first thing our little Spider remembered was being crowded with a lot of other little Spiders in a tiny brown house. This tiny house had no windows, and was very warm and dark and stuffy. When the wind blew, the little Spiders would hear it and would feel their round brown house swinging like a cradle. It was fastened to a bush by the edge of the forest, but they could not know that, so they just wiggled and pushed and ate the food that they found in the house, and wondered what it all meant.

2 They didn't even guess that a mother Spider had made the brown house and put the food in it for her Spider babies to eat when they came out of their eggs. She had put the eggs in, too, but the little Spiders didn't remember the time when they lay curled up in the eggs. They didn't know what had been nor what was to be—they thought that to eat and wiggle and sleep was all of life. You see they had much to learn.

GO ON ▶

3 One morning the little Spiders found that the food was all gone, and they pushed and scrambled harder than ever, because they were hungry and wanted more. Exactly what happened nobody knew, but suddenly it grew light, and some of them fell out of the house.

4 All the rest scrambled after, and there they stood, winking and blinking in the bright sunshine, and feeling a little bit dizzy, because they were on a shaky web made of silvery ropes. Just then the web began to shake even more, and a beautiful great mother Spider ran out on it. She was dressed in black and yellow velvet, and her eyes glistened and gleamed in the sunlight. They had never dreamed of such a wonderful creature.

5 "Well, my children," she exclaimed, "I know you must be hungry, and I have breakfast all ready for you."

6 So they began eating at once, and the mother Spider told them many things about the meadow and the forest, and said they must amuse themselves while she worked to get food for them.

7 There was no father Spider to help her, and, as she said, "Growing children must have plenty of good plain food."

8 You can just fancy what a good time the baby Spiders had. There were a hundred and seventy of them, so they had no chance to grow lonely, even when their mother was away. They lived in this way for quite a while, and grew bigger and stronger every day.

9 One morning the mother Spider said to her biggest daughter, "You are quite old enough to work now, and I will teach you to spin your web."

10 The little Spider soon learned to draw out the silvery ropes from the pocket in her body where they were made and kept, and very soon she had one fastened at both ends to branches of the bush. Then her mother made her walk out to the middle of her rope bridge, and spin and fasten two more, so that it looked like a shining cross. After that was done, the mother showed her something like a comb, which is part of a Spider's foot, and taught her how to measure, and put more ropes out from the middle of the cross, until it looked like the spokes of a wheel.

11 The little Spider got much discouraged, and said, "Let me finish it some other time; I am tired of working now."

12 The mother Spider answered, "No, I cannot have a lazy child."

13 The little one said, "I can't ever do it, I know I can't."

GO ON ▶

Chapter 5: Practice Test 1   109

14 "Now," said the mother, "I shall have to give you a Spider scolding.

15 "You have acted as lazy as the Tree Frog says boys and girls sometimes do. He has been up near the farm-house, and says that he has seen children who do not like to work. He says they were cross and unhappy children, and no wonder! Lazy people are never happy. You try to finish the web, and see if I am not right. You are not a baby now, and you must work and get your own food."

16 So the little Spider spun the circles of rope in the web, and made these ropes sticky, as all careful spiders do. She ate the loose ends and pieces that were left over, to save them for another time, and when it was done, it was so fine and perfect that her brothers and sisters crowded around, saying, "Oh! oh! oh! how beautiful!" and asked the mother to teach them. The little web-spinner was happier than she had ever been before, and the mother began to teach her other children. But it takes a long time to teach a hundred and seventy children.

 **Questions**

1. Part A

What does glistened mean as it is used in paragraph 4 of "The Little Spider"?

Ⓐ darkened

Ⓑ shined

Ⓒ closed

Ⓓ opened

Part B

Which statement best supports the answer to Part A?

Ⓐ ". . . was dressed in black . . ." (paragraph 4)

Ⓑ ". . . winking and blinking . . ." (paragraph 4)

Ⓒ ". . . gleamed in the sunlight." (paragraph 4)

Ⓓ ". . . dreamed of such a wonderful creature." (paragraph 4)

GO ON ▶

2. Part A

Why did the mother scold the little spider?

Ⓐ The little spider was not paying attention.

Ⓑ The little spider did not follow directions.

Ⓒ The little spider was being lazy.

Ⓓ The little spider was playing with her brothers and sisters.

Part B

Which detail from "The Little Spider" supports the answer to Part A?

Ⓐ "You can just fancy what a good time the baby spiders had." (paragraph 9)

Ⓑ "Let me finish it some other time; I am tired of working now." (paragraph 11)

Ⓒ "I can't ever do it, I know I can't" (paragraph 13)

Ⓓ "He says they were cross and unhappy children." (paragraph 15)

3. Part A

What is the moral of "The Little Spider"?

Ⓐ If you work hard you will finish quicker.

Ⓑ Sometimes work is hard.

Ⓒ If you work hard you will make your parents happy.

Ⓓ Hard work leads to success.

Part B
Which detail from the story best supports the answer to Part A?

Ⓐ "... You are not a baby now, and you must work and get your own food." (paragraph 15)

Ⓑ "So the little Spider spun the circles of rope in the web, and made these ropes sticky, as all careful spiders do." (paragraph 16)

Ⓒ "But it takes a long time to teach a hundred and seventy children." (paragraph 16)

Ⓓ "The little web-spinner was happier than she had ever been before, and the mother began to teach her other children." (paragraph 16)

Now, read the second story titled "The Secret" by Stephen L. Moss. Then answer questions 4 through 6.

The Secret

By Stephen L. Moss

1 Kyle crumpled another picture to throw in the wastebasket. He had been trying to draw a sports car like Uncle Lou's. But nothing he drew turned out right.

2 He noticed his teacher, Mrs. Lee, looking over his shoulder. "What's wrong, Kyle?" she asked.

GO ON ▶

3 "I want to draw a car," Kyle said. "But I can never make it look good. Is there a secret to being an artist?"

4 Mrs. Lee was silent for a moment, then said, "Yes, there is a secret. I'll tell you, but first you must do something for me."

5 "Do what?" Kyle asked.

6 "Draw that car again. Only this time, don't crumple it. Give it to me when you're done. Then, every day, do a drawing. Draw people, houses, cars, anything. Don't worry about how good the drawings are, and don't throw them away. Hand one in to me every day for four weeks. Then I'll tell you the secret."

7 "Four weeks?"

8 "Yes. It's a very important secret," said Mrs. Lee. "Draw that car. And remember, no crumpling."

9 Kyle drew Uncle Lou's car again. It didn't look right. The hood was too long, and the front wheels were bigger than the back wheels. He wanted to crumple it, but he handed it to Mrs. Lee.

10 The next day, Kyle drew his classroom's goldfish tank. He couldn't get the fish right, and the plastic treasure chest on the bottom looked crooked. He handed it in anyway.

11 Every day, Kyle drew. He drew airplanes, other kids, even Mrs. Lee. He gave all the pictures to Mrs. Lee, no matter how bad they were.

12 Kyle started to feel like drawing more. "Is it OK to do more than one picture a day?" he asked.

13 "Draw as much as you'd like," said Mrs. Lee. "The more the better."

14 Kyle began drawing at home every day. He drew Jasmine, the family poodle, and Sam, the cat. He drew Uncle Lou's car again and again.

15 Finally, four weeks had passed.

16 "Today's the day!" Kyle told Mrs. Lee.

17 "You're right," she said. "But first I want you to do one more drawing."

GO ON ▶

Chapter 5: Practice Test 1   113

18 Kyle got out his crayons and paper. He imagined Uncle Lou's car. Then he drew it. When he was finished, he showed his picture to his teacher.

19 "What do you think of it?" she asked.

20 "It's OK," he said. "It could be better."

21 "Maybe, but compare it with this one." She showed him the drawing he had done the first day.

22 Kyle looked at his old drawing, then at the one he just finished. What a difference! The new drawing wasn't perfect, but it looked a lot more like Uncle Lou's car. Kyle nodded. "But what's the secret?"

23 "It's practice. You drew every day, and look how much better your pictures got. If your work improved this much in four weeks, just think what'll happen in three months or a year."

24 Kyle looked at both drawings again. Then he handed them back to Mrs. Lee. "Would you hold on to these for another four weeks? I want to keep learning the secret."

 **Questions**

4. Part A

Read the sentence from paragraph 9 of the story.

> "He wanted to crumple it, but he handed it to Mrs. Lee."

What does the sentence show about Kyle?

Ⓐ He was angry at Mrs. Lee.

Ⓑ He got caught fooling around in class.

Ⓒ He wasn't happy with his work.

Ⓓ He was keeping his work a secret.

GO ON ▶

Part B

Which detail from "The Secret" shows another example of the answer to Part A?

Ⓐ "But I can never make it look good. Is there a secret to being an artist?" (paragraph 3)

Ⓑ "He drew airplanes, other kids, even Mrs. Lee." (paragraph 11)

Ⓒ "When he was finished, he showed his picture to his teacher." (paragraph 18)

Ⓓ "Maybe, but compare it with this one." (paragraph 21)

5. Part A

Which statement best describes what the picture adds to the story?

Ⓐ The picture shows Kyle is happy to see his drawings are improving.

Ⓑ The picture shows Mrs. Lee comparing her drawing to his.

Ⓒ The picture shows Kyle copied his drawing from a photo.

Ⓓ The picture shows that cars can be drawn different ways.

GO ON ▶

Part B
Which sentence from the story best supports the answer to Part A?

Ⓐ "Then, every day, do a drawing. Draw people, houses, cars, anything." (paragraph 6)

Ⓑ "You're right," she said. "But first I want you to do one more drawing." (paragraph 17)

Ⓒ "Kyle got out his crayons and paper. He imagined Uncle Lou's car." (paragraph 18)

Ⓓ "Kyle looked at his old drawing, then at the one he just finished. What a difference!" (paragraph 22)

6. **Complete the chart below to show how Kyle was determined to become an artist. Drag-and-drop three details from the list below into the chart. (Here, you can just write your three answer choices in the chart below.)**

Ⓐ Kyle began drawing at home every day.

Ⓑ He had been trying to draw a sports car.

Ⓒ Kyle started to feel like drawing more.

Ⓓ He drew Uncle Lou's car again and again.

Ⓔ Mrs. Lee was silent for a moment.

Details to describe that Kyle was determined to become an artist.

1.
2.
3.

GO ON ▶

Essay Question

Refer to the stories "The Little Spider" and "The Secret." Then write an essay answering question 7 below.

7. The mother spider and Mrs. Lee both try to teach important lessons to characters in the stories. Write an essay that explains how the mother spider's and Mrs. Lee's words and actions are important to the plots of the stories. Use what you learned about the characters to support your essay.

Research Simulation Task

Task Time: 75 minutes

Today you will do some research on the natural world and the processes of discovering the truth about nature. First, you will read an article titled "Ghost Ship of the Yukon Project." Then you will read an excerpt from the book *Boy, Were We Wrong About the Solar System!* As you read these sources, you will gather information and answer questions about world discoveries, so you can write a response to the essay prompt following the two readings and the questions.

First read the article "Ghost Ship of the Yukon Project." Then answer questions 8 through 11.

Ghost Ship of the Yukon Project
From *National Geographic*

About the Project

1 Led by NGS/Waitt grantee John Pollack, a small group of volunteer archaeologists and divers associated with the Institute of Nautical Archaeology (INA) is working with the Yukon government to locate and document century-old stern-wheeler wrecks dating back to the Klondike Gold Rush.

2 In 2008 the Yukon River Survey team discovered an iconic paddle wheeler, lost in 1901, in 40 feet (12 meters) of water on Lake Laberge. This small steamboat, the *A.J. Goddard*, is the sole remaining example of small stern-wheelers that were carried in pieces over mountain passes from Skagway, Alaska, to ferry men, supplies, and scows in the headwaters of the Yukon River. Prefabricated in San Francisco and Seattle, the *A.J. Goddard* was assembled on the shores of Lake Bennett during the winter of 1897–98. It foundered in a fall storm in 1901, sinking at the north end of Lake Laberge and killing three men.

3 It took more than two decades of searching by local diver Doug Davidge to find the ship, but in 2008 he and an INA team pinpointed a promising target. Davidge and Pollack returned in June 2009—just 48 hours after the ice disappeared from the site—to make the first dives ever on this wreck. They found an intact 49.9-foot (15.2-meter) vessel lying upright in 37° F (2.8° C) water.

GO ON ▶

4 The team, which includes expert archaeologists, a bush-wise local, and a professional underwater photographer, is performing a photo-inventory and will survey the ship and recommend conservation measures to the Yukon Government.

A.J. Goddard Finds

5 There was no gold on this small vessel, but there was a wealth of information as to how the rivermen of the era lived and worked. The wreck and its debris field contain a diverse collection of tools, cooking utensils, and personal effects of the crew. These artifacts appear to be the contents of a self-sufficient, working stern-wheeler on which the crew fed themselves en route and periodically had to repair their ship on a remote wilderness river. Woodworking and blacksmithing tools are abundant and include a small forge, anvil, workbench, and hand tools. Cooking gear is the second dominant category of artifact. A small cookstove is on board, and a collection of enamelware, cook pots, and bottles lie scattered around the ship. Several long bones of a large mammal were found adjacent to the ship, suggesting fresh meat was on the menu. Personal artifacts associated with the crew include boots and the remains of a coat.

6 There were clues about the ship's demise 108 years earlier. The main deck has ten hatches arranged in five pairs, and firewood is visible below deck within the forward holds. None of the hatch covers remain, suggesting they were not reliably secured and they washed away as the vessel foundered. Two axes lie on the deck at the bow where they were dropped after the crew cut away a barge in tow. One firebox door is open and stuffed with unburned wood, suggesting the men tried in vain to restart the boiler fire as the ship went down.

Work Ongoing

7 The wreck and its debris field are protected by territorial and federal law and all INA work conducted on Yukon wreck sites must be done under archaeological permit.

 **Questions**

8. Part A

What is the meaning of the word **foundered** as it is used in paragraph 2?

Ⓐ searched

Ⓑ sank

Ⓒ sailed

Ⓓ survived

Part B

Which phrase from paragraph 2 **best** helps the reader understand the meaning of **foundered**?

Ⓐ "... in a fall storm..."

Ⓑ "... killing three men..."

Ⓒ "... assembled on the shores..."

Ⓓ "... sinking at the north end..."

9. Part A

What is the **main** idea of "Ghost Ship of the Yukon Project"?

Ⓐ If you continue to work and search, you can make great discoveries.

Ⓑ The government needs to protect sunken ships.

Ⓒ The size of a ship determines its safety.

Ⓓ A boat can carry a lot of different artifacts.

GO ON ▶

Part B
Which detail from the article best supports the answer to Part A?

Ⓐ "They found an intact 49.9-foot (15.2-meter) vessel..." (paragraph 3)

Ⓑ "It took more than two decades of searching by local diver Doug Davidge to find the ship..." (paragraph 3)

Ⓒ "A small cookstove is on board..." (paragraph 5)

Ⓓ "... its debris field are protected by territorial and federal law..." (paragraph 7)

10. Part A
Which section from "Ghost Ship of the Yukon Project" introduces the process by which the divers found the ship?

Ⓐ About the Project

Ⓑ *A.J. Goddard* Finds

Ⓒ Work Ongoing

Ⓓ Both Ⓐ and Ⓒ are correct.

Part B
Which statement from the article supports the answer to Part A?

Ⓐ "In 2008 the Yukon River Survey team discovered an iconic paddle wheeler..." (paragraph 2)

Ⓑ "These artifacts appear to be the contents..." (paragraph 5)

Ⓒ "None of the hatch covers remain..." (paragraph 6)

Ⓓ "The wreck and its debris field are protected..." (paragraph 7)

GO ON ▶

11. Part A

Revisit paragraph 5. What information is learned about the rivermen who were aboard the steamboat *A.J. Goddard*?

Ⓐ The rivermen were very wealthy.

Ⓑ The rivermen were able to cook, build and fix using just sea and boat items.

Ⓒ The rivermen had a lot of clothing.

Ⓓ The rivermen were often tired while they traveled.

Part B

What phrase from paragraph 5 best supports your answer to Part A?

Ⓐ ". . . artifacts associated with the crew include boots. . ."

Ⓑ ". . . the crew fed themselves en route and periodically had to repair their ship. . ."

Ⓒ "The wreck and its debris field. . ."

Ⓓ "There was no gold on this small vessel. . ."

Read the following excerpt from the book *Boy, Were We Wrong About the Solar System!* Then answer questions 12 through 14.

Boy, Were We Wrong About the Solar System!

By Kathleen V. Kudlinski

1 Long, long ago, before people knew anything about the solar system, they saw the sun move in the sky. The moon moved, too. People watched the stars make a grand slow circle in the sky every night. But their world didn't seem to move at all.

2 They thought everything in the heavens moved around their flat, steady Earth. Boy, were they wrong!

3 We now know that we live on a little planet that moves with other worlds around a medium-size sun in a large galaxy. But it took a long time and a lot of wrong guesses to learn what we now know today.

GO ON ▶

4 Early people saw that a few stars did not twinkle. These glowing dots moved differently from all the others circling the night sky. People named these special wanderers after their gods—Jupiter, Venus, Saturn, Mercury, and Mars.

5 The moon also moved and it changed shape in the sky. Then the Earth came between the sun and the moon, it cast a round shadow on the moon. The early Greeks realized that since the Earth's shadow was round, then the Earth must be round, too.

6 People invented new tools to study the skies and measure where and when the planets moved. They made the sky maps, too, and at last saw a system to the heavens.

7 The stars, they said, were dots on a huge clear ball. Inside that glassy ball the planets and the sun occupied smaller and smaller spheres. Earth was the all-important center of everything.

8 They thought that the heavens were perfect and everlasting.

9 Boy, were they wrong about our solar system!

10 One man watched a comet slide right through where the Moon's sphere was supposed to be—and nothing happened. No glass ball shattered. The clear spheres weren't really there. The planets must just be floating through space.

11 Another astronomer saw a brand-new star appear one night. It didn't go away. Many others saw it, too. If new stars could appear, then maybe the heavens weren't unchanging.

12 A new idea came to an astronomer. He said the sun was in the center of the system, not the Earth. That would mean that we were not so important. He had no proof, so most people just laughed at the idea of a sun-centered system. Boy, were they wrong!

13 The first telescopes changed everything. Looking through them, astronomers could see that things in the heavens were not perfect, after all. The sun had spots. The moon had mountains and craters, and Saturn appeared to be lumpy.

14 And everyone could see for the first time that Venus changed shape just like our moon. That meant sunlight was shining on it from many different angles. Venus had to be circling the sun! If that was true, the other planets must be circling the sun, too. The Earth was not the center of the universe!

GO ON ▶

15 Church leaders thought these new findings went against the Bible. They had a famous scientist arrested when he wrote about the discoveries. He could never come to church again. But nothing they said could change the facts.

 **Questions**

12. Part A

What does the word cast mean as it is used in paragraph 5 of the passage?

- Ⓐ formed
- Ⓑ stopped
- Ⓒ asked
- Ⓓ disappeared

Part B

Which detail from the passage helps the reader understand the meaning of cast?

- Ⓐ "They thought. . ." (paragraph 2)
- Ⓑ ". . . round shadow. . ." (paragraph 5)
- Ⓒ "People invented. . ." (paragraph 6)
- Ⓓ "Earth was the all-important" (paragraph 7)

13. Part A

How did astronomers first learn that Earth was not the center of the universe?

- Ⓐ Astronomers looked at the old charts of comets to originally figure it out.
- Ⓑ Glass spheres helped scientists decipher planet order.
- Ⓒ They heard it from church leaders.
- Ⓓ Looking through early telescopes allowed astronomers to see that the planets revolved around the sun.

GO ON ▶

Chapter 5: Practice Test 1   125

Part B
Which detail best supports the answer to Part A?

- Ⓐ "A new idea came to an astronomer" (paragraph 12)
- Ⓑ "The sun had spots" (paragraph 13)
- Ⓒ "And everyone could see for the first time that Venus changed shape just like our moon" (paragraph 14)
- Ⓓ "Church leaders thought" (paragraph 15)

You read the article "Ghost Ship of the Yukon Project" and the excerpt from the book *Boy, Were We Wrong About the Solar System!* Think about the key details in each piece that show how curiosity contributes to discovery.

14. Write an essay comparing and contrasting the key details presented in the article and short story about discovery. Use specific details and examples from both pieces to support your ideas.

_____

_____

_____

_____

_____

_____

_____

_____

GO ON ▶

Narrative Task

Task Time: 90 minutes

Today you will read the story "The Cake Master." Pay close attention to the actions of the characters and the events in the story. Then answer the questions to help you prepare to write a narrative story in the form of a journal entry.

Read "The Cake Master." Then answer questions 15 through 20.

The Cake Master

by Carolyn Fay

1 My dad can make a cake into anything: a castle, a dragon, even a train puffing out blue-icing smoke.

2 "Evan," says my friend Jeremy, "your dad is a Cake Master."

3 "It runs in the family," I say. "Want to help me make the World's Best Cake for my dad's birthday party? My mom said I could make it while she makes the other food."

4 "Sure," says Jeremy.

5 We find a recipe and take out the ingredients: flour, sugar, butter, eggs, milk, salt, baking soda, vanilla extract, and chocolate.

6 "Why is it called 'baking soda' when it's not a drink?" asks Jeremy.

7 "I don't know."

8 "But you're the Cake Master."

9 "I'm the Cake Master, not the Ingredient Master," I say. "You're the assistant. Would you help me measure?"

10 Jeremy measures and pours.

11 I stir.

12 "Separate two eggs," Jeremy reads. "How do we do that?"

13 "We separate them from their shells, of course."

GO ON ▶

14 I crack the eggs on the edge of the bowl. The goo slides down into the batter.

15 I mix. I am a Master Mixer, too.

16 The recipe says to melt the chocolate in a double boiler. "Cake Masters don't boil double," I say. "We microwave once."

17 It gets a little messy.

18 "Need some help?" Mom asks as she makes the fruit salad.

19 "No, thanks!" I say, wiping chocolate from the countertop.

20 "Good job cleaning as you go," she says.

21 Of course. Cake Masters are tidy.

22 After stirring in the chocolate, we pour the batter into two cake pans that Jeremy smeared with butter.

23 Mom pops them into the oven.

24 We lick the spoons. We wait.

25 We peek. The two layers look brown and puffy.

26 Mom takes them out of the oven while Jeremy and I make the icing.

27 I check on the layers.

28 They're cool, but the centers have fallen. It looks like I smushed my elbow into them.

29 "Did you smush your elbow into them?" asks Jeremy.

30 "No!" I tap one layer out of the pan and onto the cooling rack.

31 "Oh no!" says Jeremy. "The cakes are ruined."

32 "No they're not," I say. "We'll fill the holes with icing."

33 Cake Masters need to be flexible. Cake Masters need to be clever. Cake Masters need a lot of chocolate icing.

34 I smear.

GO ON ▶

Chapter 5: Practice Test 1

Questions

15. Part A

What does the phrase "it runs in the family" mean in paragraph 3 of "The Cake Master"?

- Ⓐ It is difficult for the narrator, Evan, to cook.
- Ⓑ The narrator, Evan, shares common characteristics with his family members.
- Ⓒ The narrator, Evan, is a fast runner like his family members.
- Ⓓ The narrator, Evan, looks similar to his siblings.

Part B

Which two details from the first three paragraphs support the answer to Part A?

- Ⓐ ". . . help me make. . ."
- Ⓑ ". . . Your dad is a Cake Master."
- Ⓒ ". . . while she makes the other food."
- Ⓓ "We find a recipe. . ."
- Ⓔ "My dad can make. . ."

16. Part A

How do the ideas in paragraph 32 build on ideas from paragraphs 7 through 9 in "The Cake Master"?

- Ⓐ Jeremy makes a great assistant for Evan.
- Ⓑ Evan still does not know how to cook even after this process.
- Ⓒ Evan, after being confused, acts as a Cake Master, and makes the best of the situation.
- Ⓓ Evan should have asked his father for more help with this recipe.

GO ON ▶

Part B

Which two details from the passage best support the answer to Part A?

Ⓐ "Want to help. . ." (paragraph 3)

Ⓑ "Mom pops them. . ." (paragraph 23)

Ⓒ "It looks like I. . ." (paragraph 28)

Ⓓ "No they're not. . ." (paragraph 32)

Ⓔ "Cake Masters need to be flexible" (paragraph 33)

17. Part A

What is the central message of the passage from "The Cake Master"?

Ⓐ Mothers and fathers are very helpful.

Ⓑ Cooking is fun, for all ages, even kids!

Ⓒ It is very easy to make a mess when cooking.

Ⓓ It is best to remain positive and make the best of a situation.

Part B

Which detail from the passage supports the answer to Part A?

Ⓐ "But you're the Cake Master." (paragraph 8)

Ⓑ "Good job cleaning as you go. . ." (paragraph 20)

Ⓒ "The cakes are ruined" (paragraph 31)

Ⓓ "Cake Masters need to be flexible. . ." (paragraph 33)

GO ON ▶

Chapter 5: Practice Test 1   131

18. **Complete the chart based on what Evan says to his friend, Jeremy, in the passage. Drag-and-drop the details from the A–E list below that best match each description in the chart below, about how Evan reacts to each event. (Here, you can just write your answers in the chart below.)**

    Ⓐ I don't know why it's called baking soda.

    Ⓑ We'll fill the holes with icing.

    Ⓒ We peek.

    Ⓓ Measure the parts.

    Ⓔ I stir.

Event	Evan's Reaction
1) Looking at ingredients	
2) Process of cooking	
3) When cake is taken out of the oven	

19. **Part A**

    What is Evan most excited about in the process of baking the cake from "The Cake Master"?

    Ⓐ Making the cake for his father's birthday party

    Ⓑ Eating all of the icing

    Ⓒ Helping his mother with cooking

    Ⓓ Working on the cake with his friend, Jeremy

    Part B

    Which detail from the passage best supports the answer to Part A?

    Ⓐ "Want to help me make the World's Best Cake for my dad's birthday. . ." (paragraph 3)

    Ⓑ "We lick the spoons" (paragraph 24)

    Ⓒ "Mom takes them out. . ." (paragraph 26)

    Ⓓ "They're cool, but. . ." (paragraph 28)

    GO ON ▶

This story talks about Evan's father's birthday party.

20. Write Evan's journal entry about the party (as you imagine the party will happen). Include information about how the characters react throughout the story as you write the journal entry.

_____
_____
_____
_____
_____
_____
_____
_____
_____
_____
_____
_____

GO ON ▶

Chapter 5: Practice Test 1

You have reached the end of Practice Test 1.

- Review your answers.

- Then, close your book and raise your hand to turn in your work.

Practice Test 2

Literary Analysis Task

Task Time: 90 minutes

Today, you will read excerpts from two stories titled *The Thirteen Clocks* and *Charlotte's Web.* As you read, think about the actions of the characters and the events of the stories. Answer the questions to help you write an essay.

Read the excerpt from Chapter 1 of *The Thirteen Clocks.* Then answer questions 1 through 3.

The Thirteen Clocks

By James Thurber

1 Once upon a time, in a gloomy castle on a lonely hill, where there were thirteen clocks that wouldn't go, there lived a cold, aggressive Duke, and his niece, the Princess Saralinda. She was warm in every wind and weather, but he was always cold. His hands were as cold as his smile and almost as cold as his heart. He wore gloves when he was asleep, and he wore gloves when he was awake, which made it difficult for him to pick up pins or coins or the kernels of nuts, or to tear the wings from nightingales. He was six feet four, and forty-six, and even colder than he thought he was. One eye wore a velvet patch; the other glittered through a monocle, which made half his body seem closer to you than the other half. He had lost one eye when he was twelve, for he was fond of peering into nests and lairs in search of birds and animals to maul. One afternoon, a mother shrike had mauled him first. His nights were spent in evil dreams, and his days were given to wicked schemes.

2 Wickedly scheming, he would limp and cackle through the cold corridors of the castle, planning new impossible feats for the suitors of Saralinda to perform.

He did not wish to give her hand in marriage, since her hand was the only warm hand in the castle. Even the hands of his watch and the hands of all the thirteen clocks were frozen. They had all frozen at the same time, on a snowy night, seven years before, and after that it was always ten minutes to five in the castle. Travelers and mariners would look up at the gloomy castle on the lonely hill and say, "Time lies frozen there. It's always Then. It's never Now."

3 The cold Duke was afraid of Now, for Now has warmth and urgency, and Then is dead and buried. Now might bring a certain knight of gay and shining courage—"But, no!" the cold Duke muttered. "The Prince will break himself against a new and awful labor: a place too high to reach, a thing to far to find, a burden too heavy to lift." The Duke was afraid of Now, but he tampered with the clocks to see if they would go, out of a strange perversity, praying that they wouldn't.

. . .

4 The castle and the Duke grew colder, and Saralinda, as a princess will, even in a place where time lies frozen, became a little older, but only a little older. She was nearly twenty-one the day a prince, disguised as a minstrel, came singing to the town that lay below the castle. He called himself Xingu, which was not his name, and dangerous, since the name began with X—and still does. He was, quite properly, a thing of shreds and patches, a ragged minstrel, singing for pennies and the love of singing. Xingu, as he so rashly called himself, was the son of a powerful king, but he had grown weary of rich attire and banquets and tournaments and the available princesses of his own realm, and yearned to find in a far land the maiden of his dreams, singing as he went, learning the life of the lowly, and possibly slaying a dragon here and there.

5 At the sign of the Silver Swan, in the town below the castle, where taverners, travelers, tale-tellers, tosspots, troublemakers, and other townspeople were gathered, he heard of Saralinda, loveliest princess on all the thousand island of the ocean seas. "If you can turn the rain to silver, she is yours," a taverner leered.

6 "If you can slay the thorny Boar of Borythorn, she is yours," grinned a traveler.

7 "But there is no thorny Boar of Borythorn, which makes it hard."

8 "What makes it even harder is her uncle's scorn and sword," sneered a tale-teller. "He will slit you from your guggle to your zatch."

9 "The Duke is seven feet, nine inches tall, and only twenty-eight years old, or in his prime," a tosspot gurgled. "His hand is cold enough to stop a clock, and

GO ON ▶

Chapter 5: Practice Test 2   137

strong enough to choke a bull, and swift enough to catch the wing. He breaks up minstrels in his soup, like crackers."

 **Questions**

1. **Part A**

    What does scheming mean as it is used in paragraph 2 of *The Thirteen Clocks*?

    Ⓐ plotting

    Ⓑ limping

    Ⓒ performing

    Ⓓ watching

    Part B

    Which statement from paragraph 2 best supports the answer to Part A?

    Ⓐ ". . . he would limp and cackle through the cold corridors. . ."

    Ⓑ "He did not wish to give her hand. . ."

    Ⓒ ". . . the hands of all the thirteen clocks were frozen. . ."

    Ⓓ ". . . planning new impossible feats for the suitors. . ."

2. **Part A**

    What does the phrase "His hands were as cold as his smile" from paragraph 1 show about the Duke?

    Ⓐ He is emotional.

    Ⓑ He is cruel.

    Ⓒ He is afraid.

    Ⓓ He is sick.

GO ON ▶

Part B

Which detail from paragraph 1 of *The Thirteen Clocks* shows another example of the answer to Part A?

Ⓐ "He wore gloves when he was asleep. . ."

Ⓑ "He was six feet four. . ."

Ⓒ "His nights were spent in evil dreams. . ."

Ⓓ "One eye wore a velvet patch. . ."

3. **Complete the chart to show which of the Duke's behaviors show his fear of losing his niece, Saralinda, to marriage. Drag and drop three details into the chart. (Here, you can just write your three answer choices in the chart below.)**

Ⓐ He prays that time will not move.

Ⓑ He mistreats both humans and animals.

Ⓒ He makes impossible challenges for suitors.

Ⓓ He worries about the arrival of a courageous knight.

Ⓔ He wears an eye-patch.

Ⓕ He is very cold, both physically and emotionally.

GO ON ▶

Read the excerpt from Chapter 1, "Before Breakfast," of *Charlotte's Web.* Then answer questions 4 through 6.

Chapter 1: Before Breakfast
from Charlotte's Web

By E.B. White

1 "Where's Papa going with that ax?" said Fern to her mother as they were setting the table for breakfast.

2 "Out to the hoghouse," replied Mrs. Arable. "Some pigs were born last night."

3 "I don't see why he needs an ax," continued Fern, who was only eight.

4 "Well," said her mother, "one of the pigs is a runt. It's very small and weak, and it will never amount to anything. So your father has decided to do away with it."

5 "Do away with it?" shrieked Fern. "You mean kill it? Just because it's smaller than the others?"

6 Mrs. Arable put a pitcher of cream on the table. "Don't yell, Fern!" she said. "Your father is right. The pig would probably die anyway."

7 Fern pushed a chair out of the way and ran outdoors. The grass was wet and the earth smelled of springtime. Fern's sneakers were sopping by the time she caught up with her father.

8 "Please don't kill it!" she sobbed. "It's unfair."

9 Mr. Arable stopped walking. "Fern," he said gently, "you will have to learn to control yourself."

10 "Control myself?" yelled Fern. "This is a matter of life and death, and you talk about controlling myself." Tears ran down her cheeks and she took hold of the ax and tried to pull it out of her father's hand.

11 "Fern," said Mr. Arable, "I know more about raising a litter of pigs than you do. A weakling makes trouble. Now run along!"

12 "But it's unfair," cried Fern. "The pig couldn't help being born small, could it? If I had been very small at birth, would you have killed me?"

GO ON ▶

13 Mr. Arable smiled. "Certainly not," he said, looking down at his daughter with love. "But this is different. A little girl is one thing, a little runty pig is another."

14 "I see no difference," replied Fern, still hanging on to the ax. "This is the most terrible case of injustice I ever heard of."

15 A queer look came over John Arable's face. He seemed almost ready to cry himself.

16 "All right," he said. "You go back to the house and I will bring the runt when I come in. I'll let you start it on a bottle, like a baby. Then you'll see what trouble a pig can be."

17 When Mr. Arable returned to the house half an hour later, he carried a carton under his arm. Fern was upstairs changing her sneakers. The kitchen table was set for breakfast, and the room smelled of coffee, bacon, damp plaster, and wood smoke from the stove.

18 "Put it on her chair!" said Mrs. Arable. Mr. Arable set the carton down at Fern's place. Then he walked to the sink and washed his hands and dried them on the roller towel.

19 Fern came slowly down the stairs. Her eyes were red from crying. As she approached her chair, the carton wobbled, and there was a scratching noise. Fern looked at her father. Then she lifted the lid of the carton. There, inside, looking up at her, was the newborn pig. It was a white one. The morning light shone through its ears, turning them pink.

 **Questions**

4. Part A

How does Fern get her father, Mr. Arable, to change his mind about killing the runt?

Ⓐ Through rational questioning.

Ⓑ Through logical comparisons.

Ⓒ By being disrespectful to her father.

Ⓓ Both A and B are correct.

GO ON ▶

Part B
Which detail from *Charlotte's Web* supports the answer to Part A?

Ⓐ "I don't see why he needs an ax." (paragraph 3)

Ⓑ "Please don't kill it!" (paragraph 8)

Ⓒ Tears ran down her cheeks and she took hold of the ax and tried to pull it out of her father's hand. (paragraph 10)

Ⓓ "The pig couldn't help being born small, could it? If I had been very small at birth, would you have killed me?" (paragraph 12)

5. Part A
Read paragraph 14 from the story.

> "I see no difference," replied Fern, still hanging on to the ax. "This is the most terrible case of injustice I ever heard of."

What does injustice mean as used in the paragraph?

Ⓐ murder

Ⓑ inequality

Ⓒ bullying

Ⓓ lying

Part B
Which detail from the excerpt supports the answer to Part A?

Ⓐ "Please don't kill it!" (paragraph 8)

Ⓑ "But it's unfair" (paragraph 12)

Ⓒ "A little girl is one thing, a little runty pig is another." (paragraph 13)

Ⓓ "I see no difference" (paragraph 14)

GO ON ▶

6. Put in order the three events that lead to Mr. Arable's decision to keep the runt. Write your three answer choices in the box below.

Ⓐ Fern questions the difference between killing a newborn baby and a newborn pig.

Ⓑ Mrs. Arable tries to reason with Fern.

Ⓒ Fern runs after her father on the way to the hoghouse.

Ⓓ Fern screams that killing the pig is unfair.

Ⓔ Fern tries to control herself.

Ⓕ Mr. Arable leaves home with an ax.

1.
2.
3.

Refer to the excerpts from *The Thirteen Clocks* and *Charlotte's Web*. Then answer question 7.

7. The Duke and Mr. Arable both disagree with the interests of their child and niece, yet they handle their disagreements in different ways from one another.

Write an essay that explains how the Duke's and Mr. Arable's words and actions are important to the plots of the stories. Use what you learned about the characters to support your essay.

_____

_____

_____

GO ON ▶

Chapter 5: Practice Test 2

GO ON ▶

Research Simulation Task

Task Time: 75 minutes

Today you will do some research on brown bats, both those that are healthy and those that are not. First, you will read an article titled "Scientist Superheroes Fight Killer Fungus." Then you will read a story entitled "Bat Loves the Night." As you read these sources, you will gather information and answer questions about bats so you can write a response to the essay question that follows.

Read the article "Scientist Superheroes Fight Killer Fungus" from *National Geographic Kids*. Then answer questions 8 through 11.

Scientist Superheroes Fight Killer Fungus
Text from "Killer Fungus That's Devastating Bats May Have Met Its Match"

By Jane J. Lee, National Geographic Society Staff
Adapted by Allyson Shaw, National Geographic Society Staff

Introduction

1 Somebody get Batman—bats are in trouble! All over North America, the flying mammals are under attack from a deadly disease. And bad news for these creatures means trouble for people too.

2 Bats are very helpful to humans. Some species eat up pesky insects such as mosquitoes. Other species act as pollinators and seed dispersers, helping forests that have been cleared or damaged to regrow.

3 Unfortunately the bats of North America are in danger.

4 A deadly disease called white-nose syndrome has killed some seven million of them since 2006, and it continues to spread today.

Deadly Mold

5 The disease is named for the white fungus, or mold, that infects the skin on the nose, ears, and wings of hibernating bats. The fungus destroys the animals' tissue. And as they try to fight off the disease, bats wake up from hibernation and end up using more energy than they should, leading to exhaustion and starvation.

GO ON ▶

Figure 1: Little brown bats eat up pesky mosquitoes. Healthy bats means healthy humans.

Photograph by Gkuchera, Dreamstime.

From Bananas to Bats

6 Luckily some scientists are swooping into action to help save bats. These experts have developed a treatment using bacteria that's known to slow the ripening of fruits and vegetables. It does this by stemming the release of gases from fruits and vegetables that tell them to start ripening.

7 Biologist Chris Cornelison first tested the bacteria against the fungus.

8 He figured if the bacteria could prevent molds growing on bananas, it might be able to stop a mold growing on a bat.

9 And the treatment seems to be working. Bats with white-nose syndrome were captured from Missouri and Kentucky, sedated, and exposed to the bacteria.

10 Scientists then closely monitored the animals. This spring, 15 bats were declared healthy enough to be released back into the wild.

11 Scientists will continue testing the bacteria to make sure it won't harm the bats or the cave ecosystem in which they hibernate.

12 But scientists are hopeful that the treatment will protect bats throughout North America. So never mind calling Batman—thanks to some real-life superheroes, bats have a fighting chance.

GO ON ▶

 **Questions**

8. Part A

What is the meaning of the word **hibernation** as it is used in paragraph 5?

Ⓐ Sickness

Ⓑ Infection

Ⓒ Sleep

Ⓓ Destruction

Part B

What phrase from paragraph 5 helps the reader understand the meaning of **hibernation**?

Ⓐ "... leading to exhaustion..."

Ⓑ "And as they try to fight off the disease..."

Ⓒ "The fungus destroys the animals' tissue."

Ⓓ "The disease is named for the white fungus..."

9. Part A

What is the main idea of the article?

Ⓐ Scientists are working to save a creature that benefits the earth in many ways.

Ⓑ Bats get infections easily, and are in a lot of danger.

Ⓒ Scientists spend too much time working to cure infected bats.

Ⓓ Bats do more damage than good to the earth.

GO ON ▶

Part B
Which detail from the article best supports the answer to Part A?

- Ⓐ "The fungus destroys the animals' tissue." (paragraph 1)
- Ⓑ "... white-nose syndrome has killed some seven million of them since 2006..." (paragraph 4)
- Ⓒ "... 15 bats were declared healthy enough to be released back into the wild." (paragraph 10)
- Ⓓ "Scientists will continue testing the bacteria to make sure it won't harm the bats or the cave ecosystem in which they hibernate." (paragraph 11)

10. Part A
What section from the article shows the reader the ways in which scientists are working to cure infected bats?

- Ⓐ Introduction
- Ⓑ Deadly Mold
- Ⓒ From Bananas to Bats
- Ⓓ Both A and B

Part B
Which statement best supports the answer to Part A?

- Ⓐ "And bad news for these creatures means trouble for people too." (paragraph 1)
- Ⓑ "... it continues to spread today..." (paragraph 4)
- Ⓒ "And as they try to fight off the disease..." (paragraph 5)
- Ⓓ "... some scientists are swooping into action..." (paragraph 6)

GO ON ▶

11. Part A

Look at the photograph below from the article. What information is learned about bats from the photo?

Figure 1: Little brown bats eat up pesky mosquitoes. Healthy bats means healthy humans.

Photograph by Gkuchera, Dreamstime.

Ⓐ Bats are violent creatures.

Ⓑ Bats are picky eaters.

Ⓒ Bats damage the environment.

Ⓓ Bats are helpful to people.

Part B

Which words from the caption best support this?

Ⓐ "... bats eat up..."

Ⓑ "... pesky mosquitoes."

Ⓒ "... healthy humans."

Ⓓ "Little brown bats..."

Now read the second story, "Bat Loves the Night," and answer questions 12 through 14. Answering the questions will help you get ready for the Research Simulation Task.

Bat Loves the Night

By Nicola Davies

1 Bat is waking, upside down as usual, hanging by her toenails.

2 Her beady eyes open. Her pixie ears twitch.

3 She shakes her thistledown fur.

4 She unfurls her wings, made of skin so fine the finger bones inside show through.

5 Now she unhooks her toes and drops into black space. With a sound like a tiny umbrella opening, she flaps her wings. Bat is flying.

6 Out!

7 Out under the broken tile into the nighttime garden.

8 Over bushes, under trees, between fence posts, through the tangled hedge she swoops untouched.

9 Bat is as at home in the darkness as a fish is in the water. She doesn't need to see—she can hear where she is going.

10 Bat shouts as she flies, louder than a hammer blow, higher than a squeak.

11 She beams her voice around her like a flashlight, and the echoes come singing back.

12 They carry a sound picture of everything her voice has touched.

13 Listening hard, Bat can hear every detail, the smallest twigs, the shape of leaves.

14 Gliding and fluttering back and forth, she shouts her torch of sound among the trees, listening for her supper.

15 All is still . . .

GO ON ▶

16 Then a fat moth takes flight below her.

17 Bat plunges, fast as blinking, and grabs it in her open mouth.

18 But the moth's pearly scales are moon-dust slippery. It slithers from between her teeth.

19 Bat dives, nets it with a wing tip, scoops it into her mouth.

20 This time she bites hard. Its wings fall away, like the wrapper from a candy. In a moment the moth is eaten.

21 Bat sneezes. The dusty scales got up her nose.

22 A bat can eat dozens of big moths in a single night—or thousands of flies, gnats, and mosquitoes.

23 Most species of bats eat insects, but there are some that eat fruit, fish, frogs, even blood!

24 Hunting time has run out. The dark will soon be gone. In the east, the sky is getting light. It's past Bat's bedtime.

25 She flies to the roof in the last shadows and swoops in under the broken tile.

26 Inside, there are squeakings. Fifty hungry batlings hang in a huddle, hooked to a rafter by oversized feet. Bat lands and pushes in among them, toes first, upside down again.

27 Bat knows her baby's voice, and calls to it.

28 The velvet scrap batling climbs aboard and clings to Bat's fur by its coat-hanger feet.

29 Wrapped in her leather wings, the baby suckles Bat's milk.

30 Outside, the birds are singing.

31 The flowers turn their faces to the sun.

32 But inside the roof hole, the darkness stays. Bat dozes with her batling, waiting.

33 When the tide of night rises again, Bat will wake and plunge into the blackness, shouting. Bat loves the night.

GO ON ▶

Questions

12. Part A

What is the meaning of **unfurl** as it is used in paragraph 4?

- Ⓐ flaps
- Ⓑ closes
- Ⓒ taps
- Ⓓ unfold

Part B

What evidence from the text best supports your answer to Part A?

- Ⓐ ". . . hanging by her toenails." (paragraph 1)
- Ⓑ "She shakes her thistledown fur." (paragraph 3)
- Ⓒ ". . . the finger bones inside show through. . ." (paragraph 4)
- Ⓓ "Now she unhooks. . ." (paragraph 5)

GO ON ▶

13. Drag and drop three important steps in Bat's daily eating routine in order of when they occur. (Here, you can just write your three answer choices in the chart below.)

Ⓐ Bat finds her batling.

Ⓑ Bat listens for supper.

Ⓒ Bat sneezes.

Ⓓ Bat plunges.

Ⓔ Bat bites hard.

Ⓕ Bat flies to the roof.

1.
2.
3.

You have now read the article "Scientist Superheroes Fight Killer Fungus" and the story *Bat Loves the Night.* Think about the key details in each article that discuss the lives of bats.

Essay Question

14. Write an essay comparing and contrasting the key details presented in the two articles regarding different aspects of healthy and infected bats. Use specific details and examples from both articles to support your ideas.

GO ON ▶

Chapter 5: Practice Test 2

GO ON ▶

Narrative Task

Task Time: 90 minutes

Today you will read the story "John's Bright Idea." Pay close attention to the actions of the characters and the events in the story. Answer the questions to help you prepare to write a narrative story, which will conclude your work with Practice Test 2.

Read "John's Bright Idea." Then answer questions 15 through 20.

John's Bright Idea

1 Mrs. Meredith was a most kind and thoughtful woman. She spent a great deal of time visiting the poor. One morning she told her children about a family which she had visited the day before. There was a man sick in bed, his wife who took care of him, and could not go out to work, and their little boy. The little boy—his name was Bernard—had interested her very much.

2 "I wish you could see him," she said to her own children, John, Harry, and Clara, "he is such a help to his mother. He wants very much to earn some money, but I don't see what he can do."

3 After their mother had left the room, the children sat thinking about little Bernard.

4 "I wish we could help him to earn money," said little Clara.

5 "So do I," said Harry.

6 For some moments John said nothing, but, suddenly, he **sprang** to his feet and cried: "I have an idea!"

7 The other children also jumped up all attention. When John had an idea, it was sure to be a good one.

8 "I tell you what we can do," said John. "You know that big box of corn Uncle Sam sent us for popping? Well, we can pop it, and put it into paper bags, and Bernard can take it round to the houses and sell."

9 When Mrs. Meredith heard of John's idea, she, too, thought it a good one.

GO ON ▶

Chapter 5: Practice Test 2   155

10 Very soon the children were busy popping the corn, while their mother went out to buy the paper bags. When she came back, she brought Bernard with her.

11 In a short time, he started out on his new business, and, much sooner than could be expected, returned with an empty basket.

12 Tucked into one of his mittens were ten nickels. He had never earned so much money before in his life. When he found that it was all to be his, he was so delighted he could hardly speak, but his bright smiling face spoke for him. After he had run home to take the money to his mother, John said: "We have corn enough left to send Bernard out ever so many times. May we do it again?"

13 "Yes," said Mrs. Meredith, "you may send him every Saturday morning, if you will pop the corn for him yourselves. John, will you agree to take charge of the work?"

14 "Indeed I will," replied John, and he kept his word. For many weeks, every Saturday morning, no matter what plan was on foot, no matter how good the coasting or skating, he saw that the corn was all popped, the paper bags filled, and arranged in the basket when Bernard arrived.

15 People began to watch for the "little pop-corn boy," and every week he had at least fifty cents to take home, and often more. And all this was because of John's bright idea, and the way he carried it out.

 **Questions**

15. Part A
What does the phrase **sprang** mean in paragraph 6 of "John's Bright Idea"?

Ⓐ John lies down to think about his idea.

Ⓑ John thinks quickly!

Ⓒ John leaps out of his seat.

Ⓓ John remains sitting.

GO ON ▶

Part B

Which two details from the first few paragraphs support the answer to Part A?

- Ⓐ "but, suddenly . . ."
- Ⓑ ". . . had interested her very much."
- Ⓒ ". . . to his feet . . ."
- Ⓓ "There was a man sick in bed."
- Ⓔ "I wish we could help him . . ."

16. Part A

How do the ideas in paragraphs 1 through 5 build on ideas from paragraphs 6 through 9 in "John's Bright Idea"?

- Ⓐ Mrs. Meredith's community shares similar feelings about helping those in need.
- Ⓑ Mrs. Meredith's children are introduced.
- Ⓒ Mrs. Meredith explains that she is having a hard time thinking of an idea.
- Ⓓ Mrs. Meredith explains about the hard times of Bernard before the children think of ways to help him.

Part B

Which two details from the passage best support the answer to Part A?

- Ⓐ "He is such a help to his mother . . ." (paragraph 2)
- Ⓑ "I wish we could help him to earn money." (paragraph 4)
- Ⓒ "He saw that the corn was all popped . . ." (paragraph 14)
- Ⓓ ". . . arranged in the basket . . ." (paragraph 14)
- Ⓔ "People began to watch for the 'little pop-corn boy' . . ." (paragraph 15)

GO ON ▶

Chapter 5: Practice Test 2   157

17. Part A
What is the central message of the passage from "John's Bright Idea"?

Ⓐ It is important to work together to help others in need.

Ⓑ Children can come up with helpful ideas!

Ⓒ Children can be hard workers, too!

Ⓓ Family is an important part of a community.

Part B
Which detail from the passage supports the answer to Part A?

Ⓐ ". . . but, suddenly, he sprang to his feet . . ." (paragraph 6)

Ⓑ ". . . returned with an empty basket. (paragraph 11)

Ⓒ "After he had run home to take the money to his mother . . ." (paragraph 12)

Ⓓ "And all this was because of John's bright idea, and the way he carried it out." (paragraph 15)

18. Complete the chart based on Mrs. Meredith's initial talk with her children. Drag and drop three details that describe how the children react to each event. (Here, you can just write your three answer choices in the chart below.)

Ⓐ Excited to be given the opportunity.

Ⓑ Shop for pop-corn to sell.

Ⓒ Begin to think about ways to help.

Ⓓ Comes up with the idea to sell the pop-corn.

Ⓔ Finds neighbors to help.

Children in Story	Reactions
1. Clara and Harry	
2. John	
3. Bernard	

GO ON ▶

19. Part A

How does the community respond to the selling of pop-corn by Bernard in the story, "John's Bright Idea"?

Ⓐ The community is worried because they do not know Bernard very well.

Ⓑ The community prefers other food besides pop-corn.

Ⓒ The community does not like pop-corn.

Ⓓ The community is very happy and excited about the new pop-corn selling business.

Part B

Which detail from the passage best supports the answer to Part A?

Ⓐ " 'Indeed I will,' replied John . . ." (paragraph 14)

Ⓑ ". . . he saw that the corn was all popped, the paper bags filled, and arranged in the basket when Bernard arrived." (paragraph 14)

Ⓒ "People began to watch for the 'little pop-corn boy,' and every week he had at least fifty cents to take home, and often more." (paragraph 15)

Ⓓ "And all this was because of John's bright idea, and the way he carried it out. (paragraph 15)

This story talks about the beginning of Bernard's new pop-corn business, with the help of Clara, Harry, and John.

20. Think about Bernard's new pop-corn community business. Decide what might happen next in the story if the pop-corn business continues to succeed! Include information about how the characters react throughout the story as you write what happens next.

_____

_____

_____

GO ON ▶

You have reached the end of Practice Test 2.

- Review your answers.

- Then, close your book and raise your hand to turn in your work.

CHAPTER 6

Answer Keys: Practice Tests 1 and 2

Practice Test 1

Literary Analysis Task

1. **Part A: B**

    Explanation: The answer here is B because the story tells us that the mother spider's eyes are glistening in the sunlight, which is another way of saying that her eyes are shining. This is why "shined" would be the best option here.

    Standard: RL.3.4 Determine Meaning of Words

    Part B: C

    Explanation: As we examined in Part A, since the sun is shining, it makes the mother spider's eyes glisten. Since "gleaming" is similar to "glisten," answer choice C "gleamed in the sunlight" is the best answer to support our response to Part A.

    Standard: RL.3.1 Demonstrate Understanding of a Text

2. **Part A: C**

    Explanation: Paragraphs 12–14 show us the mother spider speaking to her daughter. We see that the daughter spider wants to wait to finish her work, but the mother encourages her not to be lazy, which is answer choice C.

    Standard: RL.3.3 Character Description

Part B: B

Explanation: Answer choice B shows us the daughter spider talking about how she does not want to work on the web creation anymore. This makes the mother scold her daughter.

Standard: RL.3.1 Demonstrate Understanding of a Text

3. **Part A: D**

   Explanation: Most of this fun story consists of the interactions between the mother spider and her daughter, which by the end of the story show that hard work in creating webs is important, which is answer choice D.

   Standard: RL.3.2 Central Idea

   Part B: D

   Explanation: Answer choice D shows us how happy this hard work makes the daughter spider, which directly links to the concept of hard work leading to success.

   Standard: RL.3.1 Demonstrate Understanding of a Text

4. **Part A: C**

   Explanation: Because Kyle wanted to crumple his work and throw it out in this paragraph, this quote shows that he was not happy with his work, which is answer choice C.

   Standard: RL.3.1 Demonstrate Understanding of a Text

   Part B: A

   Explanation: Answer choice A shows Kyle's frustration when he shares with his teacher that he can never make his artwork look good.

   Standard: RL.3.1 Demonstrate Understanding of a Text

5. **Part A: A**

   Explanation: At this point of the story, Kyle is beginning to progress with his artwork. In this picture, Kyle is smiling, so answer choice A, expressing Kyle's happiness, is the best answer.

   Standard: RL.3.7 Illustrations in Context

Chapter 6: Answer Keys (Practice Test 1)

Part B: D

Explanation: Answer choice D shows how Kyle sees the difference in his new work, after much practice, in comparison with his old work, and the difference is a positive one!

Standard: RL.3.1 Demonstrate Understanding of a Text

6. **A, C, D**

    Explanation: Answer choices A, C, and D all directly show Kyle's determination to be a better artist. Not only was Kyle drawing a lot when he was home, but he also enjoyed drawing cars, a pastime inspired by his Uncle Lou.

    Standard: RL.3.1 Demonstrate Understanding of a Text

7. See PARCC® Grade 3 Rubric for Literary Analysis Task in Appendix B at the back of this book.

    Standard: RL.3.6 Point of View; RL.3.9 Compare and Contrast Themes; W.3.2 Write Explanatory Texts

Research Simulation Task

8. **Part A: B**

    Explanation: The last sentence in paragraph 2 mentions a storm and that the steamboat sank in the storm, which directly links to answer choice B.

    Standard: RL.3.4 Determine Meaning of Words

    Part B: D

    Explanation: The word "sinking" in answer choice D directly relates to the storm, and to the key word "sank" mentioned in Part A of this question, making it the best answer choice to support our answer to Part A.

    Standard: RI.3.1 Demonstrate Understanding of a Text

9. **Part A: A**

   Explanation: While a great deal happened in this story, the underlying theme is that it is because of great exploration that discovery can occur—which is the message in answer choice A.

   Standard: RI.3.2 Central Idea

   Part B: B

   Explanation: Answer choice B explains that it took over two decades to make such a discovery, which links directly to our theme in Part A.

   Standard: RI.3.1 Demonstrate Understanding of a Text

10. **Part A: A**

    Explanation: The title of this section of the article shows us that an overview (about the project) is about to be given, which is why answer choice A is the best choice, since this section gives the reader a summary of the project itself.

    Standard: RI.3.8 Describe Logical Connections

    Part B: A

    Explanation: Answer choice A describes an introductory discovery of the Yukon River Survey team, which is part of the summary of the project. This is why answer choice A directly relates to Part A.

    Standard: RI.3.1 Demonstrate Understanding of a Text

11. **Part A: B**

    Explanation: Answer choice B directly connects to the detailed information about the steamboat and its crew that we learn from reading paragraph 5.

    Standard: RI.3.1 Demonstrate Understanding of a Text

    Part B: B

    Explanation: The details in answer choice B directly support the detailed summary found in Part A of this question. Answer choice B is the only answer that supports Part A.

    Standard: RI.3.1 Demonstrate Understanding of a Text

Chapter 6: Answer Keys (Practice Test 1)

12. **Part A: A**

    Explanation: Because of the movement of the moon, a shadow began to exist and was created. Answer choice A is the best option because the word "formed" is closely related to "created."

    Standard: RL.3.4 Determine Meaning of Words

    Part B: B

    Explanation: Not only is answer choice B a direct quote from the same paragraph as the word in Part A ("cast"), but also this quote connects to the shape of the shadow from the moon.

    Standard: RI.3.1 Demonstrate Understanding of a Text

13. **Part A: D**

    Explanation: Answer choice D discusses cause and effect – that astronomers learned of the relationship between the planets and the sun through investigation and by looking through a telescope. In this way, they were able to determine that Earth revolved around the sun. As the passage makes clear, with this new information in hand, early astronomers basically redrew the known universe. They pinpointed its center at or near the sun. What we know today as the sun-centered solar system, they knew as the universe. Today we know that the universe contains many solar systems. Nothing beyond our own "neighborhood" could be seen by 17th-century astronomers.

    Standard: RI.3.1 Demonstrate Understanding of a Text

    Part B: C

    Explanation: To support our answer to Part A, answer choice C in Part B shows an exact lesson learned by looking through the telescope. That makes it our best answer choice.

    Standard: RI.3.1 Demonstrate Understanding of a Text

14. See PARCC Grade 3 rubric for Research Simulation Task in Appendix B at the back of this book.

    Standard: RI.3.6 Distinguish Point of View; RL.3.9 Compare and Contrast Themes; W.3.2 Write Informative Texts

Narrative Task

15. Part A: B

   Explanation: Answer choice B shows us how the narrator, Evan, is much like his family members in his cooking skills.

   Standard: RL.3.4 Determine Meaning of Words

   Part B: B, E

   Explanation: Because we know that Evan is talking about his family, answer choices B and E directly relate to his family members, especially his dad, who is referenced in both of these answer choices.

   Standard: RL.3.1 Demonstrate Understanding of a Text

16. Part A: C

   Explanation: Answer choice C shows the change in Evan, from being initially confused to understanding his cooking and baking of the cake. Since this sort of shift and growth happens in Evan from these specific paragraphs, this sort of shift also has to be shared in answer choice C, as well.

   Standard: RL.3.5 Chronology of Reading

   Part B: D, E

   Explanation: Because we are looking for responses that support the idea of Evan changing, we can see that answer choices D and E talk about this shift and growth in Evan.

   Standard: RL.3.1 Demonstrate Understanding of a Text

17. Part A: D

   Explanation: Although Evan struggled at first, he had to stay positive in order to grow and succeed. Answer choice D states just this, and is the most accurate answer to this question.

   Standard: RL.3.2 Central Idea

Chapter 6: Answer Keys (Practice Test 1)

Part B: D

Explanation: Answer choice D is direct advice on how Evan can grow as a Cake Master himself. Specifically, he needs to be flexible and open in order to be better at his craft.

Standard: RL.3.1 Demonstrate Understanding of a Text

18. 1) A, 2) D, 3) B

    Explanation: Evan reacts to each of these three events in the story. Three answer choices (A, D, B) move us through the story, from hesitation and uncertainty to specific responses.

    Standard: RL.3.5 Chronology of Reading

19. **Part A: A**

    Explanation: Evan wants to make his father proud, which is a repeated theme throughout this story. Answer choice A specifically talks about Evan's father, which makes this the best answer choice.

    Standard: RL.3.1 Demonstrate Understanding of a Text

    Part B: A

    Explanation: Answer choice A directly relates to Evan's father's birthday, which supports our response to Part A.

    Standard: RL.3.1 Demonstrate Understanding of a Text

20. See PARCC® Grade 3 Rubric for Narrative Writing Task in Appendix B at the back of this book.

    Standard: RL.3.6 Point of View; RL.3.9 Compare and Contrast Themes; W.3.3 Write Narratives

Practice Test 1—Writing Task Essay Maps

Literary Analysis Task

Here's what you were asked: The mother spider and Mrs. Lee both try to teach important lessons to characters in the stories. Write an essay that explains how the mother spider's and Mrs. Lee's words and actions are important to the plots of the stories. Use what you learned about the characters to support your essay.

How well did you answer the question? Let's review what you needed to do and take a look at a model response that would earn a top score.

Provide an introduction.	The mother spider's and Mrs. Lee's words and actions helped to encourage their loved ones to work hard towards success.
State a clear purpose or theme.	Hard work pays off.
Provide details to support the main idea.	In the story, "The Little Spider's First Web," the mother spider encourages her children to see how hard work turns into the creation of a beautiful web! After her children begin to see the web forming, the mother spider repeats to her children that it is important to continue through a job even if we are tired. When the daughter spider states that she is tired, the mother spider urges her daughter to continue working towards the making of a silvery web. Like the spider story, "The Secret" also shows us how hard work pays off, as we can see through the actions between Mrs. Lee, the teacher, and Kyle, the student. Kyle wants to learn how to draw a car, but is discouraged at his very first draft. Mrs. Lee reminds Kyle that he must keep trying over and over until he gets it right. After many tries, Kyle notices great improvement in the way that he has drawn the car, and is very happy about his artwork.
Stay focused on the purpose of the texts.	While one text shows that hard work pays off by not stopping our task, the other encourages in a different way, focusing on the importance of trying over and over again to meet success.
Provide a conclusion.	Both texts tell us about lessons in working hard, either through continuing through our work or trying again. Whichever advice we receive, it is important to take this advice and try the best that we can.

Research Simulation Task

Here's what you were asked: Write an essay comparing and contrasting the key details presented in the article and short story about discovery. Use specific details and examples from both pieces to support your ideas.

How well did you answer the question? Let's review what you needed to do and take a look at a model response that would earn a top score.

Provide an introduction.	Different types of discovery are exciting and help us to find out new information.
State a clear purpose or theme.	Why is discovery so important, and what can we learn from being curious?
Provide details to support the main idea.	The article, "Ghost Ship of the Yukon Project," tells the story of a ship that was found. In finding this ship, we learn about the history of where the ship came from, and also, we learn about the people, culture, and times of the early 1900s! The ship that was found gave scientists and explorers many clues to understand life in the past. Scientists and explorers found artifacts and objects that would help them figure out what life was like during the time that this ship still sailed. In *Boy, We Were Wrong About the Solar System*, we learn about how the scientific discovery of planets came about! By using different inventions, we were able to learn more about the solar system. Scientists and astronomers used sky maps and telescope technology to learn about stars, planets, and how the solar system worked.
Stay focused on the purpose of the texts.	While one text helps us see how artifacts can give us clues about history and life of past years, the second text tells how technology advancement helped scientists change their way of thinking about the solar system.
Provide a conclusion.	It is important to follow our curiosity in looking for new information. Through the finding of clues and using technology to find even more clues, we should always be thinking about different possibilities!

Narrative Task

Here's what you were asked: Write Evan's journal entry about the party (as you imagine the party will happen). Include information about how the characters react throughout the story as you write the journal entry.

How well did you answer the question? Let's review what you needed to do and take a look at a model response that would earn a top score.

Provide an introduction.	I'm Evan and I want to tell you about my father's birthday party that we just had today! My friend, Jeremy, and I worked on a cake to serve for my father on this day also!
State a clear purpose or theme.	We could not wait to see the cake that we had made for my father. Not only was my mom excited, but we were also excited to surprise my dad!
Provide details to support the main idea.	All of my father's friends showed up at our house, and it was very sunny out. Everyone was happy, and my father played card games with his friends. Even some of my friends came too! Jeremy and I put on some more decorations on the cake to make it extra special for dad. We not only put on interesting icing, but we also used different colors to spell out my dad's name, and even put candles into the cake. We could not wait to share the cake with the party!
Stay focused on the purpose of the texts.	Because the cake did not look like a normal cake, Jeremy was nervous. I told him that it was really cool looking, and that we should be confident and proud of our work in making this delicious cake for my dad!
Provide a conclusion.	My mother played the music, and began singing happy birthday. Everyone joined in! As I walked out with the cake from the kitchen, everyone smiled and clapped with happiness. My dad looked down at the cake, blew out his candles, and thanked me for my hard work, and shouted that he could not wait to have a slice!

Practice Test 2

Literary Analysis Task

1. **Part A: A**

   Explanation: Answer choice A speaks to the direct word in this sentence that links to "scheming," which is "planning." The best answer choice that is closest to "planning" is "plotting."

   Standard: RL.3.4 Determine Meaning of Words

   Part B: D

   Explanation: Of these answer choices, answer choice D gives us a word that is similar to "scheming" and "plotting" (as referenced above in question No. 1), which is "planning," so answer choice D would be the best selection.

   Standard: RL.3.1 Demonstrate Understanding of a Text

2. **Part A: B**

   Explanation: Often, when someone is referred to as "cold," they are mean. Another for mean is "cruel," which is found in answer choice B.

   Standard: RL.3.3 Character Description

   Part B: C

   Explanation: The only answer choice that directly connects with something that is mean or cruel, as mentioned in Part A, is answer choice C, which mentions the Duke's "evil dreams."

   Standard: RL.3.1 Demonstrate Understanding of a Text

3. **A, C, D**

   Explanation: The three of these answer choices A, C, and D show the Duke's fear and worry asked about in this question. All other answer choices do not directly reflect this fear and worry.

   Standard: RL.3.1 Demonstrate Understanding of a Text

4. **Part A: D**

   Explanation: Fern's rational questioning and logical comparisons both directly affect her father in changing his mind about the runt. This is a question for which you must be very careful to read all the answers, or you might miss that there are *two* correct answers, A and B, as mentioned in the correct answer choice D.

   Standard: RL.3.1 Demonstrate Understanding of a Text

   Part B: C

   Explanation: Answer choice C shows how Fern makes the argument to her father. She makes the comparison between the birth of the runt and her own birth, asking questions to help persuade her father.

   Standard: RL.3.1 Demonstrate Understanding of a Text

5. **Part A: B**

   Explanation: It is clear that Fern is not happy with her father, and by using comparison, she states that she is not happy because her father's response to the runt is unfair. This word, "injustice," is also similar to unequal, which is linked to "inequality."

   Standard: RL.3.4 Determine Meaning of Words

   Part B: B

   Explanation: Answer choice B uses the word "unfair," which is very similar to "inequality" and "injustice," which makes this the best answer choice of those listed for this question.

   Standard: RL.3.1 Demonstrate Understanding of a Text

6. **C, D, A**

   Explanation: Each of these three events leads to Mr. Arable's decision to spare the runt. It is through Fern's arguing and reasoning to her father, including each of these logical steps, that Mr. Arable moves from his decision to do away with the small pig to his decision to save it.

   Standard: RL.3.5 Chronology of Reading

Chapter 6: Answer Keys (Practice Test 2)

7. See Grade 3 PARCC® rubric for Literary Analysis Task in Appendix B at the back of this book.

    Standard: RL.3.6 Point of View; RL.3.9 Compare and Contrast Themes; W.3.2 Write Explanatory Texts

Research Simulation Task

8. **Part A: C**

    Explanation: Answer choice C is best because it is the direct opposite of the word used in the sentence of paragraph 5, "bats wake up. . ." Since bats wake up from hibernation, hibernation can be viewed as similar to sleep.

    Standard: RL.3.4 Determine Meaning of Words

    Part B: A

    Explanation: Answer choice A talks about "exhaustion," which means extremely tired. Because the bat is extremely tired, it leads to hibernation, which is connected closely to our answer in Part A of this question.

    Standard: RI.3.1 Demonstrate Understanding of a Text

9. **Part A: A**

    Explanation: We see in our reading of this article that these bats benefit the earth in many different ways, and as a result, scientists are working on methods in which they can help save this creature. As a result of the theme of this reading, answer choice A is the best selection.

    Standard: RI.3.2 Central Idea

    Part B: D

    Explanation: Answer choice D links directly to our answer in Part A, as well as our explanation for choosing our answer for Part A. Specifically, bats are viewed as important in this article, and scientists focus on helping this creature, which is expressed in the quote of answer choice D.

    Standard: RI.3.1 Demonstrate Understanding of a Text

10. **Part A: C**

   Explanation: Answer choice C lists the section from this article, "From Bananas to Bats," which directly links to the comparison and experimentation between bacteria in fruits and bacteria on bats.

   Standard: RI.3.3 Relationships Amongst Text

   Part B: D

   Explanation: Here, only one answer choice directly links to the actions taken by scientists to help cure these creatures. In answer choice D, scientists are "swooping into action," which connects with the question in Part A.

   Standard: RI.3.1 Demonstrate Understanding of a Text

11. **Part A: D**

   Explanation: It is important with this question to not only look at the picture, but to also read the caption for it, which mentions ways in which bats are helpful. Answer choice D speaks to the ways in which bats can help the environment.

   Standard: RI.3.7 Illustrations in Context

   Part B: C

   Explanation: The phrase "healthy humans" in answer choice C helps to support the point that bats can help the environment, and as a result, other species besides only themselves.

   Standard: RI.3.1 Demonstrate Understanding of a Text

12. **Part A: D**

   Explanation: The image conveyed by the words in this paragraph is one of the bat awakening, and part of that process is the unfolding of her wings, as explained in answer choice D. You can picture the bat waking up and stretching out her wings.

   Standard: RL.3.4 Determine Meaning of Words

Chapter 6: Answer Keys (Practice Test 2)

Part B: C

Explanation: Because the bat's bones show through, this information supports our answer to Part A in that by unfolding the bat's wings, other features of the bat are then exposed. Answer choice C serves to be the best answer in supporting our response to Part A of this question.

Standard: Standard: RI.3.1 Demonstrate Understanding of a Text

13. **B, D, E**

Explanation: In the reading, it is clear that the bat follows three specific steps when looking for food: listening for supper, plunging and swooping down to catch the supper, and then biting into the food for capture. These three steps are described in the correct answer choices B, D, and E.

Standard: Standard: RI.3.1 Demonstrate Understanding of a Text

14. See PARCC® Rubric for Research Simulation Task in Appendix B at the back of this book.

Standard: RI.3.6 Distinguish Point of View; RL.3.9 Compare and Contrast Themes; W.3.2 Write Informative Texts

Narrative Task

15. **Part A: C**

Explanation: Answer choice C shows the character, John, leaping. As we can read in paragraph 6, John's movement is sudden, which directly links to springing or leaping, which makes answer choice C the correct answer here.

Standard: RL.3.4 Determine Meaning of Words

Part B: A, C

Explanation: It is the suddenness and the movement itself onto John's feet that help to add context to our answer choice about the meaning of "sprang" in Part A. Answer choices A and C in Part B describe the way in which John moves, as well as the result (onto his feet), both of which are helpful in defining "sprang."

Standard: RL.3.1 Demonstrate Understanding of a Text

16. **Part A: D**

   Explanation: In between paragraphs 1–5 and 6–9, a shift occurs in the story. First we learn of the hard time of Bernard, and then the children begin to want to help Bernard based on this information. Answer choice D reveals the relationships between both pieces of the plot.

   Standard: RL.3.5 Chronology of Reading

   Part B: A, B

   Explanation: Answer choices A and B directly link to the information shared about Bernard, as well as the need to help Bernard after learning about this information. While other answer choices are also connected to this part of the story, these two details link to our answer to Part A the best.

   Standard: RL.3.1 Demonstrate Understanding of a Text

17. **Part A: A**

   Explanation: Answer choice A is the most fitting when talking about the central idea of this story. The children want to help Bernard, and this is the right thing to do. This sort of idea is repeated throughout the short story.

   Standard: RL.3.2 Central Idea

   Part B: D

   Explanation: In answer choice D, we read again about John's bright idea. This idea is connected closely to helping Bernard, which is also linked to the theme we have identified in Part A of this question.

   Standard: RL.3.1 Demonstrate Understanding of a Text

18. **C, D, A**

   Explanation: Based on our reading, we can use direct details to link the children's responses to the event at hand. Different children react differently, all contributing towards helping Bernard, as found through answer choices C, D, and A.

   Standard: RL.3.5 Chronology of Reading

Chapter 6: Answer Keys (Practice Test 2)

19. Part A: D

Explanation: As is the theme for most of this short story, not only are the children willing to help Bernard, but the community is also very excited to help. Answer choice D is the best because of this clear fact.

Standard: RL.3.1 Demonstrate Understanding of a Text

Part B: C

Explanation: Of all the answer choices, C connects to the community's positive response to Bernard. With this sort of response, Bernard sees the money that the community has donated to him.

Standard: RL.3.1 Demonstrate Understanding of a Text

20. See PARCC® Rubric for Narrative Task in Appendix B at the back of this book.

Standard: RL.3.6 Point of View; RL.3.9 Compare and Contrast Themes; W.3.3 Write Narratives

Practice Test 2—Writing Task Essay Maps

Literary Analysis Task

Here's what you were asked: The Duke and Mr. Arable both disagree with the interests of their child and niece, yet they handle their disagreements in different ways from one another. Write an essay that explains how the Duke's and Mr. Arable's words and actions are important to the plots of the stories. Use what you learned about the characters to support your essay.

How well did you answer the question? Let's review what you needed to do and take a look at a model response that would earn a top score.

Provide an introduction.	When working through disagreements, it is important to notice how our reactions can affect outcomes!
State a clear purpose or theme.	The Duke and Mr. Arable both work through disagreements in very different ways. It is important to think about the ways that we work through disagreements with the people around us.
Provide details to support the main idea.	Through these two excerpts, we learn about two very different disagreements. We learn, most of all, that it is important to think about other people when making our decisions, but we also learn a lot about fairness in coming to an agreement in reading both of these stories. Looking at different disagreements, as we see in these two texts, it is interesting to see how we may respond in different ways, and how those responses can change an entire story.
Stay focused on the purpose of the texts.	While the Duke provides the man with an almost impossible chance to win over his niece, we also see the strength in Mr. Arable's daughter's points. The Duke says that the man would need to beat a boar to meet with his niece, but this boar does not even exist. This makes any fixing of the disagreement to be impossible. Mr. Arable, on the other hand, listens to his daughter, who says that the baby pig is still a meaningful life, and says that this life is important. This argument saves the pig, and makes the pig a part of the family!
Provide a conclusion.	In looking at different disagreements, I think it is best to look at both sides of the problem to see what is the best solution for everyone involved.

Chapter 6: Answer Keys (Practice Test 2)

Research Simulation Task

Here's what you were asked: Write an essay comparing and contrasting the key details presented in the two articles regarding different aspects of healthy and infected bats. Use specific details and examples from both articles to support your ideas.

How well did you answer the question? Let's review what you needed to do and take a look at a model response that would earn a top score.

Provide an introduction.	Bats are amazing creatures, but disease has killed millions of them.
State a clear purpose or theme.	Scientists are working to save the bats, but why should we care?
Provide details to support the main idea.	The article "Scientist Superheroes Fight Killer Fungus" shows the steps being taken to fight the disease and save the bats. The disease is actually a fungus that infects the bats' skin and eats away at their tissue. Saving the bats is important not only to preserve the balance of nature but also to help humans. The story "Bat Loves the Night" helps take the mystery out of bats by showing us up close how they live. For example, bats have highly developed hearing to let them know where they are – a good thing since they are active in the darkness.
Stay focused on the purpose of the texts.	While one text helps us see the threat to bats, the other text helps us see what bats do like no other animal. For example, in just one night's work, a bat can eat "dozens of big moths…or thousands of flies, gnats, and mosquitoes." And who wants mosquitoes biting them and possibly spreading disease? The bats also help spread the seeds that allow damaged forests to grow back.
Provide a conclusion.	I'm glad that scientists have found a way to help the bats so the bats can continue to help us and help the earth.

Narrative Task

Here's what you were asked: Think about Bernard's new pop-corn community business. Decide what might happen next in the story if the pop-corn business continues to succeed. Include information about how the characters react throughout the story as you write what happens next.

How well did you answer the question? Let's review what you needed to do and take a look at a model response that would earn a top score.

Provide an introduction.	The Saturday pop-corn selling business continued to be a success for Bernard.
State a clear purpose or theme.	Bernard helped his mother with paying bills for the family. He also became very good friends with Clara, Harry, and John.
Provide details to support the main idea.	Soon, the business became an even bigger success! Bernard kept on working hard and the pop-corn deliveries became an everyday practice for Bernard.
Stay focused on the purpose of the texts.	As the business became popular, and Bernard tried out new flavors of pop-corn, Bernard asked for the help of his friends. Once again, John had a bright idea! John suggested to Bernard that they should make different sizes of the pop-corn bags, and raise the price because of the product's popularity. The business boomed! Sales increased and the pop-corn business became a shared business between Bernard and John. Clara and Harry joined the company as workers to help with sales. Different flavors of the pop-corn made the community enjoy the pop-corn even more, and with the chance to buy pop-corn every single day, more and more people liked the business in town.
Provide a conclusion.	John and Bernard continue working towards brighter ideas, and won't just stop at pop-corn sales.

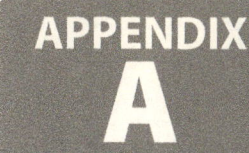

Graphic Organizers and Charts

Literary Analysis and Research Simulation Graphic Organizer

Source #1 Notes	Source #2 Notes

Note-taking T-Chart

Character	Lesson	Words	Actions

Appendix A: Graphic Organizers and Charts

Literary Analysis and Research Simulation Compare/Contrast Graphic Organizer:

Venn Diagram

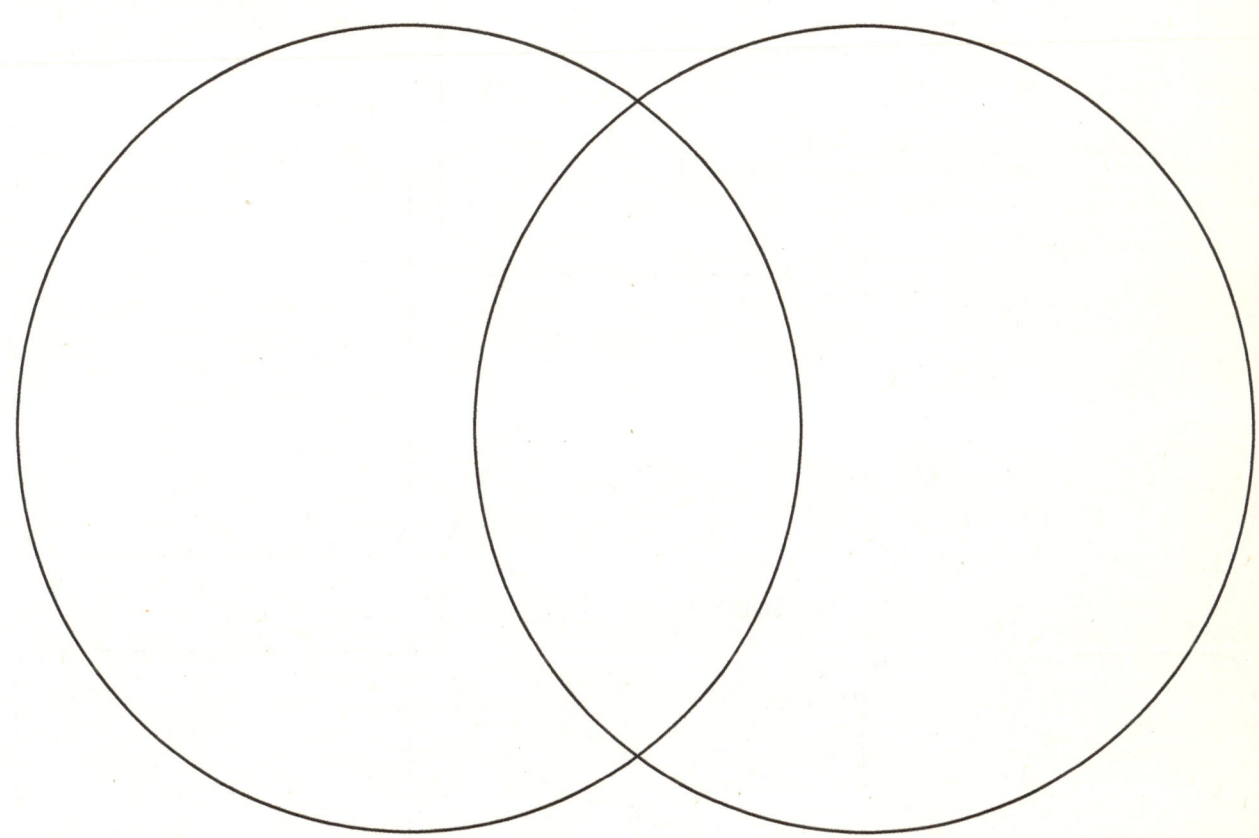

Video Clip Note-taking Graphic Organizer

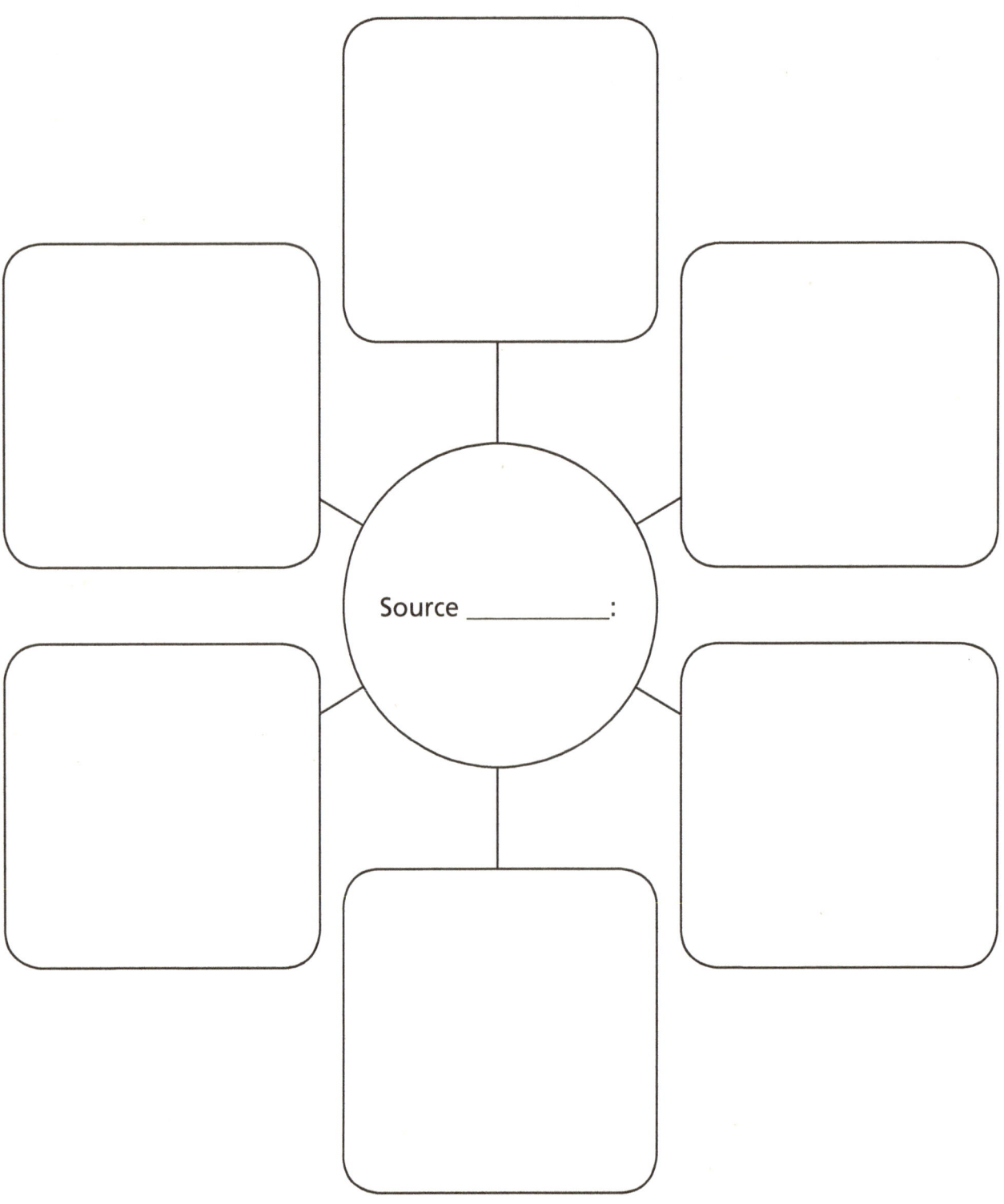

Source Relationships Graphic Organizer

Topic:		
Source A	**Source B**	**Source C**
How do the sources work together?		

Story Graphic Organizer

Beginning of Story ⬇	
Middle of Story ⬇	
Ending	

Appendix A: Graphic Organizers and Charts

Story Pyramid

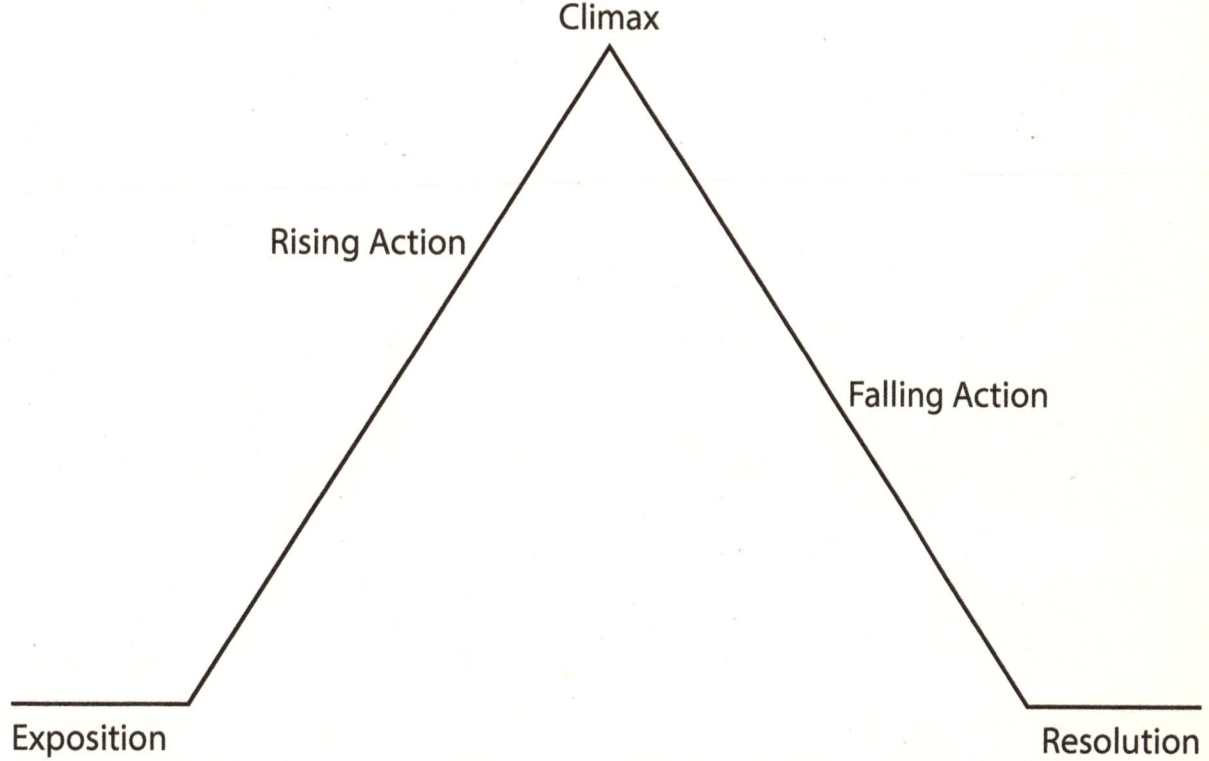

APPENDIX B

PARCC® Literary Analysis, Research Simulation, and Narrative Rubrics

> **Note to Educators and Parents:** The following rubrics will help you explain to your students/children the level of achievement that is expected of them in their writing in the PARCC® exam. These rubrics are published by PARCC® and are aligned to the Common Core ELA/Literacy Standards. As you practice the writing tasks in this book with students, be sure to take time to simplify these rubrics to make sure the achievements are understood.

GRADE 3
CONDENSED SCORING RUBRIC FOR PROSE CONSTRUCTED RESPONSE ITEMS
(Revised July 29, 2014)*

Research Simulation Task (RST) and Literary Analysis Task (LAT)

Construct Measured	Score Point 3	Score Point 2	Score Point 1	Score Point 0
Reading Comprehension of Key Ideas and Details	The student response demonstrates **full comprehension** by providing an **accurate** explanation/ description/ comparison and by referencing the texts explicitly.	The student response demonstrates **comprehension** by providing a **mostly accurate** explanation/ description/comparison and by referencing the text(s) explicitly.	The student response demonstrates **limited comprehension** and **may** reference the text(s) explicitly.	The student response does not demonstrate comprehension of the text(s).
Writing Written Expression	The student response • addresses the prompt and provides **effective** development of the topic that is **consistently appropriate** to the task by using **clear** reasoning and **relevant, text-based** evidence; • **consistently** demonstrates **purposeful and controlled** organization; • uses language to express ideas with clarity.	The student response • addresses the prompt and provides **some** development of the topic that is **generally appropriate** to the task by using reasoning and **relevant, text-based** evidence; • **generally** demonstrates **purposeful and controlled** organization; • uses language to express ideas with **some** clarity.	The student response • addresses the prompt and provides **minimal** development of the topic that is **limited in its appropriateness** to the task by using **limited** reasoning and **text-based** evidence; **or** • is a developed, text-based response with **little or no awareness** of the prompt; • demonstrates **purposeful** organization that **sometimes is not controlled**; • uses language to express ideas with **limited** clarity.	The student response • is **undeveloped** and/or **inappropriate** to the task; • demonstrates **little or no** organization; • does not use language to express ideas with clarity.
Writing Knowledge of Language and Conventions	The student response to the prompt demonstrates **full command** of the conventions of standard English at an appropriate level of complexity. There **may** be a **few minor errors** in mechanics, grammar, and usage, but **meaning is clear**.	The student response to the prompt demonstrates **some command** of the conventions of standard English at an appropriate level of complexity. There **may** be errors in mechanics, grammar, and usage that **occasionally impede understanding**, but the **meaning is generally clear**.	The student response to the prompt demonstrates **limited command** of the conventions of standard English at an appropriate level of complexity. There **may** be errors in mechanics, grammar, and usage that **often impede understanding**.	The student response to the prompt demonstrates **no command** of the conventions of standard English. **Frequent and varied errors** in mechanics, grammar, and usage **impede understanding**.

* This rubric is subject to further refinement based on research and study.

Appendix B: PARCC® Literary Analysis, Research Simulation, and Narrative Rubrics

Narrative Task (NT)

Construct Measured	Score Point 3	Score Point 2	Score Point 1	Score Point 0
Writing Written Expression	The student response • is **effectively** developed with narrative elements and is **consistently appropriate** to the task;	The student response • is developed with **some** narrative elements and is **generally appropriate** to the task;	The student response • is **minimally** developed with **few** narrative elements and is **limited in its appropriateness** to the task;	The student response is **undeveloped** and/or **inappropriate** to the task;
	• **consistently** demonstrates **purposeful and controlled** organization;	• demonstrates **purposeful and controlled** organization;	• demonstrates **purposeful** organization that **sometimes is not controlled**;	• demonstrates **little or no** organization;
	• uses language to express ideas with clarity.	• uses language to express ideas with **some** clarity.	• uses language to express ideas with **limited** clarity.	• does not use language to express ideas with clarity.
Writing Knowledge of Language and Conventions	The student response to the prompt demonstrates **full command** of the conventions of standard English at an appropriate level of complexity. There may be a **few minor errors** in mechanics, grammar, and usage, but **meaning is clear**.	The student response to the prompt demonstrates **some command** of the conventions of standard English at an appropriate level of complexity. There **may** be errors in mechanics, grammar, and usage that **occasionally impede understanding**, but the **meaning is generally clear**.	The student response to the prompt demonstrates **limited command** of the conventions of standard English at an appropriate level of complexity. There **may** be errors in mechanics, grammar, and usage that **often impede understanding**.	The student response to the prompt demonstrates **no command** of the conventions of standard English. **Frequent and varied errors** in mechanics, grammar, and usage **impede understanding**.

NOTE:

- The reading dimension is not scored for elicited narrative stories.
- Per the CCSS, narrative elements in grades 3-5 may include: establishing a situation, organizing a logical event sequence, describing scenes, objects or people, developing characters personalities, and using dialogue as appropriate.
- The elements of organization to be assessed are expressed in the grade-level standards W1–W3.

A response is considered unscoreable if it cannot be assigned a score based on the rubric criteria. For unscoreable student responses, one of the following condition codes will be applied.

Coded Responses:

A = No response; B = Response is unintelligible or undecipherable; C = Response is not written in English; E = Refusal to respond; F = Don't understand/know.

Rubrics reprinted with permission of, and copyright © by, PARCC Inc.

APPENDIX C

PARCC® Technology and Accessibility

Technology of the PARCC® Exam

If you plan to have your students take the computer-based version of the PARCC® test, they may be faced with unfamiliar online technology. The PARCC® exam uses a variety of online navigational tools and interactive response models in its computerized version. To prepare students to use these online tools and resources, educators and parents may wish to spend some time guiding students in a practice online test on the PARCC® website, in addition to working through this book. You can find PARCC® practice tests here: http://www.parcconline.org/assessments/practice-tests.

Special Education/Accommodations

The PARCC® consortium has released a *PARCC Accommodations Manual 4.0*, which outlines five categories of accommodations available to students with disabilities intended to provide "equitable access" to the tests:

- Presentation accommodations include allowable changes in the method or format in which the test or test questions are provided to the student. These may include, for example, the use of Braille or sign interpretation of test items.

- Response accommodations include allowable changes in the method used by the student to provide responses to test questions. These may include dictating responses to a scribe or using a Braille note-taker.

- Timing and scheduling accommodations include extending the duration of time allowed for testing, allowing a student to take frequent breaks, or [allowing a student] to take the test at a certain time of day.

- Setting accommodations include changes to the location or conditions in which the test is administered, including separate location or group size.

- Special-access accommodations include accommodations that expand access to the test for a small number of students with disabilities in the areas of reading, writing, and calculating who require additional supports and meet certain criteria, as noted by the IEP/504 plan teams.

There are also a number of universal design elements and accessibility features that will be available to all students, either by the student's choice or at the discretion of a school. Those features include computerized pop-up glossaries, spell-checkers, a highlighting tool, page-flagging, or magnification.

APPENDIX D

Acknowledgments and Credits

Chapter 2

Pg. 10: "My Father Meets a Lion" from *My Father's Dragon* by Ruth Stiles Gannett. New York: Random House, 1948. Public domain.

Pg. 16: "The One-Eyed Giant" from *Tales from the Odyssey* by Mary Pope Osborne, New York: Hyperion, 2003. "The One-Eyed Giant" text copyright © 2002 by Mary Pope Osborne.

Pg. 20: "A Bat Is Born" by Randall Jarrell from *The Complete Poems* by Randall Jarrell. Originally published by Farrar, Straus and Giroux, LLC, copyright © 1969, renewed 1997 by Mary von S. Jarrell.

Pg. 25: From "Tops and Bottoms" by Janet Stevens. Text and illustrations copyright © 1995 by Janet Stevens.

Pg. 32: "How the Camel Got His Hump" by Rudyard Kipling. Copyright © 1897 by the Century Company. Public domain.

Chapter 3

Pg. 50: "Plant Life Cycles," by Anita Ganeri (2005, Heinemann-Raintree).

Pg. 62: Excerpt from *Animal Life Cycles: Growing and Changing* by Bobbie Kalman, New York: Crabtree Publishing Company. Copyright © 2006 Crabtree Publishing Company.

Pg. 65: "The Rise of Machu Picchu," by Kristin B. Rattini. From "City in the Sky," National Geographic Kids; June/July 2015, Issue 451, p22. Copyright © National Geographic Society.

Pg. 67: "The Secrets of Stonehenge," by Kristin B. Rattini, National Geographic Kids; June/July 2008, Issue 381, p34. Copyright © National Geographic Society.

Pg. 73: "Ooh ... Orcas!" Published in *Ranger Rick*, March 2015, Vol. 49 Issue 3, pg. 6. Copyright © National Wildlife Federation.

Pg. 76: "Everyone Wants to Know About Sharks," by Kathy Kranking, published in *Ranger Rick*, June/July 2015, copyright © National Wildlife Federation.

Pg. 80: "Mission Animal Rescue: Beaver," by Scott Elder, National Geographic Kids; Feb. 2015. Copyright © National Geographic Society.

Pg. 83: "Mission Animal Rescue: Bald Eagle," by Kitson Jazynka, National Geographic Kids; July 2015. Copyright © National Geographic Society.

Chapter 4

Pg. 93: "Was It a Dream?" by Edith Robarts, from *Laugh and Play: A Collection of Original Stories*, n.d., New York: E.P. Dutton & Co. Public domain.

Chapter 5

Pg. 107: "The Little Spider's First Web" from *Among the Meadow People* by Clara Dillingham Pierson, copyright © 1897 E.P. Dutton & Co. Public domain.

Pg. 111: "The Secret," by Stephen L. Moss, copyright © 2014 Highlights for Children, Inc., Columbus, Ohio. All rights reserved. Reprinted by permission. Illustrations by Peter Bay Alexandersen.

Pg. 118: "Ghost Ship of the Yukon Project" copyright © National Geographic Society and National Geographic Partners, LLC. All rights reserved.

Pg. 122: "Boy, Were We Wrong About the Solar System!" by Kathleen V. Kudlinski, Copyright © 2008 by Kathleen V. Kudlinski. Published in the United States by Dutton Children's Books, a Penguin Random House company.

Appendix D: PARCC® Acknowledgments and Credits

Pg. 127: "The Cake Master," by Carolyn Fay, copyright © 2013 Highlights for Children, Inc., Columbus, Ohio. All rights reserved. Reprinted by permission.

Pg. 135: Excerpt from *The Thirteen Clocks*, by James Thurber, copyright © 1950 by James Thurber. New York: The New York Review of Books.

Pg. 139: "Before Breakfast" from *Charlotte's Web*, by E.B. White. Copyright © 1952 by E.B. White. Copyright renewed 1980 by E.B. White.

Pg. 144: "Scientist Superheroes Fight Killer Fungus" from "Killer Fungus That's Devastating Bats May Have Met Its Match." Copyright © National Geographic Society and National Geographic Partners, LLC. All rights reserved.

Pg. 149: "Bat Loves the Night," by Nicola Davies, copyright © 2001 by Scholastic, Inc.

Pg. 154: "John's Bright Idea" adapted by Polk Bros. Foundation Center for Urban Education, DePaul University. Public domain.

Notes